Fifth Avenue, New York (1908) The year of the author's birth. (New York
Public Library — Picture Collection)

HERMAN G. WEINBERG

A MANHATTAN ODYSSEY

A Memoir

ANTHOLOGY FILM ARCHIVES
New York 1982

Copyright © 1982 by Herman G. Weinberg
Library of Congress Catalogue Card Number: 82-074157
Printed in the United States of America

ISBN-0-911689-09-5 (paper)
ISBN-0-911689-10-9 (cloth)
ISBN-0-911689-11-7 (paper set)

ACKNOWLEDGMENTS

Grateful acknowledgment is made:

To Film Culture (Jonas Mekas, editor-publisher) for reprints by permission of *A Visit With Hans Richter*, Dec. 1951, *Some Footnotes to the Arts*, January 1960, *Coffee, Brandy & Cigars*, January 1963, and, in slightly different form, *San Francisco*, 1960.

To The National Enquirer for permission to reprint *Arlene Dahl: Love is the Best Beauty Treatment*, Sept. 19, 1978.

To the Belwin Mills Publishing Corp. for permission to reprint the lyrics of the chorus of the song, *Take Me In Your Arms* (composer/arranger: Rotter, Parish, Markush). Copyright © 1932 by Mills Music, Inc. Copyright renewed. All Rights Reserved.

To Larry Spier, Inc., Music Publishers, for permission to reprint two lines from the song, *If You Knew Susie* (by B.G. De Sylva and Joseph Meyer). Copyright © JoRo Music Corp., New York, N.Y.

To Harcourt Brace Jovanovich, Inc. for permission to reprint passages from *Reflections* by Walter Benjamin.

To Classic Film/Video Images (formerly Classic Film Collector) for permission by Sam K. Rubin, editor, to reprint Patsy Ruth Miller's statement on Picasso from the Issue No. 41 of The Classic Film Collector.

To The New York Times for permission to reprint the except by Nelson Bryant, © 1974 by The New York Times Company. (From his column on unicorns in the Dec. 8, 1974 issue.)

To MPL Communications Inc. for permission to reprint the lyrics of the chorus of the song, *Yes My Darling Daughter* (words and music by Jack Lawrence). © 1940 Leo Feist, Inc. © Renewed 1968 by MPL Communications, Inc. International Copyright Secured. All Rights Reserved.

To the W.W. Norton Company, Inc. for permission to reprint the passage from *The Street Where I Live* by Alan Jay Lerner.

To Margaret Tsuda for permission to reprint her poem, *Night Sailing*, copyrighted by her in 1972. Originally published in the Christian Science Monitor.

To the Welk Music Group for permission to reprint the lyrics of the chorus of the song, *Who*, by Jerome Kern, Otto Harbach and Oscar Hammerstein II. Copyright © 1925 by the Harms Company, Santa Monica, California. Copyright Renewed. International Copyright Secured. All Rights Reserved.

To Warner Bros. Music for permission to reprint excerpts from the lyrics of the following songs:

Bei Mir Bist Du Schön (Means That You're Grand). English Version by Sammy Cahn and Saul Chaplin. Original lyric by Jacob Jacobs. Music by Sholom Secunda. © 1937 (Renewed) by Warner Bros. Inc. All Rights Reserved.

Kiss Me Again (Lyric by Henry Blossom. Music by Victor Herbert.) © 1915 (Renewed) Warner Bros. Inc. All Rights Reserved.

Smiles (Lyric by J. Will Callahan. Music by Lee S. Roberts) © 1917 (Renewed) Warner Bros. Inc. All Rights Reserved.

April Showers (Lyric by B.G. DeSylva. Music by Louis Silvers) © 1921 (Renewed) Warner Bros. Inc. All Rights Reserved.

To the W.W. Norton Company, Inc. for permission to reproduce the photo of Mount Vernon Place, Baltimore, by Aubrey Bodine.

To The Pace Gallery, New York, for the information that the drawing by Picasso of Ethel and Julius Rosenberg, dedicated and given to their sons, "is in the public domain, as far as we know. It does not belong to the (Picasso) family."

To Gretchen

In ancient times, a knight carried his lady's colors of her scarf with him into battle — to bring him luck, to preserve him for her. For the same reasons I dedicate this book to you.

A NOTE TO THE READER

Everyone who writes a memoir adds another facet to the world. By now it is a multi-faceted globe spinning away for whatever reason, whose days, months, years, are divided in many different ways—dark shadows mingling with the light, not just Edward Fitzgerald's "checker boards of nights and days," but those "untold consequences of dark and vari-colored things" of which Pasternak speaks.

A memoir is an attempt, while in the process of setting down the things one remembers—that is, in choosing *which* of those things to set down—to rationalize one's life, to give it a *raison d'être*, in the hope that the total recounting will add up to something more than just the sum of its parts. Else why should someone else be interested in it? The mathematical principles behind the mysteries of the pyramid of Cheops and Stonehenge are more interesting than these phenomena as works of art. Thus it is with the telling of a life, that what memory decants will have at its core some revelations, some universal truths besides the anecdote.

"Reminiscences," said Walter Benjamin, "even extensive ones, do not always amount to an autobiography . . . For autobiography has to do with time, with sequence, and what makes up the continuous flow of life . . . . of moments and discontinuities. For even if months and years appear . . . . it is in the form they have at the moment of recollection . . . " Yet I hope to have achieved an autobiography in my own way by a combination of "time, sequence and the continuous flow of life" and "moments of discontinuities"—the former in the first half of the book, the latter in the second half. In both, however they appear, "the moment of recollection" slots things recollected as accurately as it can be. In the first half, they fall into place chronologically; in the second they form not only my own "remembrance of things past," the morals of which are still present, but are also concerned with that present. In any case, they are meant to reflect the truth.

Yet that mercurial and quicksilver thing, truth, is an elusive thing, even when you are hell-bent on telling it—or think you're telling it, which is probably why Pilate didn't wait for an answer to his query, "What is truth?" The best thing about the Japanese film, *Rashomon,* is just this — that it poses the question.

Truth is so often what you want it to be, what indeed, you feel it *must* be . . . .

Von Sternberg, in his project for a film that never got made—*The Temptation of Luther Eustace,* from Shelby Foote's novel of the deep South, *Follow Me Down*—sought also to pose the same question. If I knew the answer for myself, I might not have felt impelled to embark on this book. It is in the hope of finding out, what will reveal itself in the telling, that I have undertaken it, for myself, and, I hope, for the reader.

I have two thoughts to sustain me in that hope—one from Pascal (*Pensées,* X)—"We arrive at the truth not by reason alone but also by the heart"—and Blake (*The Marriage of Heaven and Hell*)—"Everything possible to be believed is an image of the truth." Freud even zeroed in on it when he wrote, in a letter to Arnold Zweig in 1936, "Biographical truth is unattainable and even if one were to attain it one could not make much use of it." What are we to make of that?

In a sense, all work is a memoir, my own previous books (there are some half dozen of them) have already revealed myself, for "all work is autobiographical if it is serious," as Tennessee Williams observed. "Everything a writer produces is sort of his inner history, transposed into another time"—whether the subjects be whatever they be—cabbages or kings — in my case the search for an aesthetic (if there is one) where the art of the cinematograph was concerned.

Books are temporal things, some more than others, some less, but in some way, for all their variegated kind, they add up. (Who said you couldn't add different things?) I love them all and they have been, as much as anything else, my life. James Huneker once said he could bear anything except the thought of leaving his books*

Didn't Charles Lamb once say, at a time when the making of books was among the noblest professions of mankind, that before opening a book one ought to pause for a moment—and say grace?

---

*"I weep sometimes at the thought of dying," he said, "for in that great inane I shall not have my books . . ." *(The Intimate Letters of James Gibbon Huneker)*

I used to say, "A library, anywhere, is my second home." I liked its quietude, its smell of books (there *is* a "library smell"), the fact that you could rest your weary head on your folded arms in a brief nap on the library table (where a girl might be reading Fran Lebowitz or Erica Jong, or maybe even Virginia Woolf, the while wondering how they let people sleep in libraries)—not conspicuously, to be sure, but in some remote nook (you can, can't you?)—a moment's refuge from an all-too-clamorous world.

And yet, in the last analysis (which is every writer's refuge), George Herbert, that gentlest of 17th century poets, was right—"Years know more than books," he said. More even than *Don Quixote,* I'd say, or even *A Guide to the Perplexed*—aye, even *The Catcher in the Rye.* Yet here I am with another book, withal, as if there were not enough in the world—more than anyone would ever have time to read (so many good ones are there)—being a record of some of those years from a clump of fifty, if you please, as I saw them, as much as I can now crystallize them, can now put them into words. Fifty—from 1928 to 1978. No, I'll start even earlier—1919. Can you stand it? Nor will I hazard a guess that the reader may find here thoughts that even Cervantes, Maimonides or Salinger may not have thought of first—perish the thought!

But the years that have accumulated to make up my own biblical "threescore and ten" have revealed aspects to me of the world I never knew existed, though if one had the wit "to catch on" early in life as to "what it was all about," one needn't have waited that long. (Beverly Nichols wrote his autobiography at 25.) These aspects I hope to share with the reader. They say that, having reached this age, everything from now is "pure gravy"—but since gravy is proscribed in my diet, I don't even have that. What, then, am I left with? Since I've no answer to that, I must get on with the telling of it . . . .

First, let me quote Erica Abeel, herself the author of an autobiography, and a good one, too, *Only When I Laugh* (meaning by that, of course, that's when the memory of what she went through hurt her). "I think," she said, "that autobiography imposes a decorum." Of course, by its very nature. I will try to be guided by that.

Now, on with it . . . . "Sing in me," too, "Muse, and through me tell the story of that man . . . . the

wanderer . . . . "* like we all are—wanderers—on the journey
through life . . . .

*Homer, *Odyssey*.

The City is the teacher of the man.

Plutarch

Manhattan, because most of it happened
here — and, when it happened elsewhere, I saw it
through the "prism" which Manhattanites always
carry with them.

Write, Josephine, you must write . . .

The way *you* see things, not the way
others talk about them when they speak
of what they have seen . . . You know how
to see things and much that is fabulous-
ly true will be within your vision if
you keep it pure. Those sights will not
only then come within the range of your
eyes, they must settle there, as the snow
must fall on northern lands. Because it
is the untold consequences of dark and
vari-colored things that make the eyes
what they are . . . our eyes depend on those
things as the sun depends on dragon flies,
not vice-versa . . .

—Boris Pasternak (in a
letter to his twelve-
year-old sister)

REQUIESCAT

Tread lightly, she is near
  Under the snow,
Speak gently, she can hear
  The daisies grow.

All her bright golden hair
  Tarnished with rust,
She that was young and fair
  Fallen to dust.

Coffin-board, heavy stone,
  Lie on her breast.
I vex my heart alone
  She is at rest.

Peace, peace, she cannot hear
  Lyre or sonnet,
All my life's buried here,
  Heap earth upon it.

OSCAR WILDE
On the death of his
little sister, and
in memory of my own.

SYLVIA (1919)

The wonderful thing about children is that they don't really need anything except to know that they are loved. Of course, you must sustain them, too, with food and shelter, but this can be of the simplest. They'll make do with anything as long as you're there, and your embrace is warmer than any blanket. How touching it is to see how resourceful they are at play, even when they have nothing. A large empty cardboard packing box makes a fine house and, if it has flaps, so much the better, then it has doors and windows, too. We used to play a game with chairs in the living room, after dinner and before bedtime. The chairs were placed in a row, one behind the other—in this way they made a train and, as there were four of us—Sylvia, Max, Arthur and me—Sylvia, Max and I were passengers and Arthur was the conductor collecting tickets and answering questions ("Is there a diner ahead?" "No, it's two cars back.") In those days we made frequent trips between New York and

Buffalo, where we had uncles and cousins. We didn't eat in the diner, though—mother's cold veal sandwiches from her basket of provisions were delicious. But when we played "trains," in order to make it more realistic, we asked if there was a diner ahead and when dinner would be served. Sometimes Arthur would play a double role and come through imitating the dining chimes of the dining-car porter that everyone knew so well:

Then one day a strange man was in the house when I got back from school. He followed father into Sylvia's bedroom and I caught a glimpse of her sitting up in her bed. I thought I saw white cotton in her nostrils. How could she breathe? I thought. Maybe I was mistaken—still how could she . . . ? What had happened so suddenly? I only remember bits and pieces from now on . . . Obviously, Sylvia was sick . . . she'd been stricken with something. What? No one said anything, if they knew. How many days passed? I don't remember. I was looking out our front window, though I saw nothing, when I heard a scream . . .

"D a d d e e e!" It was Sylvia.

It was Sylvia reaching out her arms for help before something pulled her down into an abyss from which she would never see us again.

She hadn't strength for a second cry—her last contact with life—but if only father could run to her and pull her back indeed with his arms from whatever it was that was tearing her away from him.

Oh, he ran to her . . .

And then he came out. It was quiet now. He had no expression at all on his face. He just dropped. If a chair had not been there where he dropped, he would have fallen to the floor. So he sat there for some moments and I tried to hide in a dark corner of the room (the lights hadn't been turned on). Then it wasn't as of he had started crying, but—how can I describe it?—as if he had resumed crying from a time before . . . a distant time long ago . . .

"Mamaleh," mother used to call her. Yiddish for "little

mother"—and now she would never grow up to be a mother.

Have you ever seen a man cry?

It's a terrible thing. It's as if all the values, everything in the world, were suddenly without value. All the fine words and the fine buildings and the republic, even God himself, were without value, without meaning. What did they do to help her?

I did not understand this then—I was 11 and that's not much. She wasn't even 11. She must have been 9 or 10, the age of Oscar Wilde's little sister, Isola, who died after her tenth birthday. Maybe it was the pandemic of "Spanish flu," which we called it at the time—1919—against which school children were protected by wearing little gauze bags around their necks containing camphor, which were distributed in all the schools. But hadn't she also been so protected? I remember I didn't cry. Children don't cry when one of their kind dies—they have not lost the protection and love that sustains them. This they feel instinctively. But if a parent dies, then all hell breaks loose. I'm speaking of young children. I think that what I'm saying is generally true. I know it was true for me.

In the days that followed I noticed that the lid of the upright piano we had was not only closed but the sheet music always stacked there was no longer there. She was the only one among us that was taking music lessons and I remembered how she used to regale us with "The Wild Horseman" from Schumann's "Album for the Young," the one that goes . . .

I noticed, too, that a silhouette of her profile that we had done of her once at a fair, and which we had framed and hung by the piano on the wall, was now turned to the wall. One day I was asked to go with father to the synagogue. As we walked silently together I saw that the lapel on the jacket of his suit was rent—torn, as if purposely ripped. It was only years later that I learned it was a Jewish ritual of mourning.

"It is raining in the village," wrote Verlaine, *"it is raining in my heart . . ."*

"Let this be witness to the world that my heart is torn," said my father's torn garment.

"Did he break into tears?" asked Shakespeare. "There are no truer faces than those so washed . . ."

In the synagogue, word had been brought to the rabbi that my father wished to say Kaddish, and in the hushed silence that followed, I heard for the first time those terrible words, those final words that are said to commemorate the dead, words with which I was to become familiar, over and over again, as the years passed and took their toll, one by one . . .

Yisgadal, v'yiskadash, sh'mey raboh
B'olmoh divrusay b'richu . . .

I have no pictures of either her or father. Their absence from among my things is something like what Melville must have meant when he said that there were true places which were not to be found on any map . . . indeed, he said, they were the truest . . .

(To Jimmy Green, with whom I first looked "beyond the blue horizon.")

THE TWENTIES 1919-1929

"Life, with all its Chinese lanterns . . . "
—*GEORGE JEAN NATHAN*

Well, and then there was Newark, first for me into that blithe era—the Twenties. No one writes about Newark and for good reason. Orson Welles once described Los Angeles as "two Newarks" and that probably does it. Once I have recalled the bronze sculpture of Lincoln by Saint-Gaudens in the downtown area, I'm finished. Of course there was the Branford Theatre, which I also recall, but that was just a movie theatre, altho' where I saw some of my first films—Hall Caines' *The Christian*, Winston Churchill's *The Inside of the Cup*, Wesley Barry in *Dinty*, James W. Gerard's *My Four Years in Germany* ("America won't fight, eh?" repeats the American Ambassador to the German Kaiser in 1917), Clara Kimball Young in *Hush* (compare that to one of our own age's film titles, *Grease*), Guy Bates Post in *Out of the Fog*, Gaston Glass, Alma Rubens and Vera Gordon in *Humoresque*, Louise Glaum in *The Tiger Woman*, William Farnum in *The Last of the Duanes*, Elsie Janis in a recruiting film for the armed forces, a film about the youth of Lincoln, another about the war with Mexico, my first Chaplins, and then *Foolish Wives*. It was the latter which got me on "the movie track" (as it did Jean Renoir when he first saw it in Paris, following which he abandoned ceramics for the cinema and made it his very own, as much as anyone else ever did, beginning with his extraordinary *Nana*, starring his wife, Catherine Hessling, a film which could have been signed by von Stroheim.)

The Twenties—as if life was the movies! A time remembered as if the days were of blue and gold . . . .

When Marilyn Miller in the Otto Harbach-Jerome Kern musical, "Sunny," was lighting up the New York stage with:

Who stole my heart away?
Who makes me dream all day?
Dreams I know can never be true,
Seems as though I'll ever be blue—
Who means my happiness?
Who would I answer "Yes" to
Well, I ought to guess who—
No one but you!

—and Eddie Cantor was loping across the Broadway stage with:

If you knew Susie, like I know Susie,
Oh, oh, oh, what a girl . . . .

—and Al Jolson was singing about *April Showers* "that bring the flowers that bloom in May"—

It's not raining rain, you know,
it's raining violets . . . .

—and the night was rife with *Naughty Riquette, The Chocolate Soldier* and *Mlle. Modiste:*

Sweet summer breeze,
    whispering trees,
Stars shining softly above—
Roses in bloom,
    wafted perfume,
Sleeping birds dreaming of love . . . .

—compare that to this age's rock and roll—and, fragrant with sweet aloes of the old songs, *Whispering, Three O'Clock in the Morning, Who Can Tell?* from *Apple Blossoms, Blue Skies,* and *Smiles . . . .*

There are smiles that make us happy,
There are smiles that make us blue,
There are smiles that steal away the
    tear-drops,
As the sunbeams steal away the dew . . .
There are smiles that have a tender
    meaning,
That the eyes of love alone may see,
But the smiles that fill my life with
    sunshine
Are the smiles that you give to me!

—note how sweet they were, how they were all love songs, in the purest sense . . . such as the song with the refrain, "I'll never smile again until I smile at you . . . ." — while, on the other hand, Percy Hammond, reviewing a new musical for the Herald-Tribune, was saying:
"In re-reading my review, I notice that I have knocked everything except the chorus girls' knees, and there the good Lord anticipated me."

When Jim Apperson (Jack Gilbert) in *The Big Parade* throws his shoe to Melisande from the truck carrying him away from her in the insane military confusion of troops moving up to the front lines, so she'd have a souvenir of him, the audience wept . . . A half century later when I showed this scene to my film students at The City College in New York they laughed . . .

—An era of which George Jean Nathan was to say, years later to a young friend, "The era that blossomed here was alive with silver bells . . . and there were magic lanterns and there were girls and there was the night. The wondrous lovely madness of the night went out of American life with the Twenties. You're a lucky man if you got a taste of it. I was luckier—I got more."

While all this was going on, my family was in Newark where my father ran a men's shop (haberdasher's we called it then) and it was there I met Tuppy. Tuppy was sales clerk for us in the shop and, being I was an avid listener, he used to tell me tales of his service in the British Expeditionary Forces during World War I. He'd been a sapper. "A bloke's got to be out of his mind to take a job like that," he said. "It was bloody awful, laying mines—Ypres, Mons, the Somme, Soissons, Vimy Ridge . . . I came out of it by sheer luck, nothing else. But what about the blokes that didn't come out, eh? What about them? For king and country my arse!" Then with a straight face he'd add—"The noise! And the people!" He would recite some of the songs (unexpurgated versions) the British Tommies used to sing during their marches. *Tipperary*, of course, but that bit of doxology that began (to the tune of "Mademoiselle from Armentiers"):

Praise God from whom all blessings flow,
Parlez-vous,
Man wants but little here below,
Parlez-vous . . . .

. . . . or the one that went . . . .

The French they are a funny race,
Parlez-vous,
The French they are a funny race,
Parlez-vous,
They fight with their feet and they . . .

which is as far as I dare take it in a book designed (I hope)
for a wide general readership . . . . but they all ended:

Hinky-dinky parlez-vous!

He came from the West Midlands of England, he said, and
once boasted he could speak in Old Saxon until his cockney got
in the way and garbled it all up.

"Mlle. from Armentiers" was taken up by the American
doughboys but they all had their own—the French had
Madelon, of course, and the British had theirs with the
retorical question the English Tommies asked their girls:

O who's been here afore me, lass,
And how did he get in?

—while in the course of his service and brief leaves in London,
he said, he met Stacy Aumonier and Wilfred Owen . . . .

"Red lips are not so red
As the stained stones kissed
by England's dead . . . . "

. . . . he would intone. And then, overcome by emotion he
once broke out with, "Oh, the world, the world! What a place
you are!"

He remembered the regatta at Cowes in the August of '14, as
full of bunting flapping in the breeze as ever, but now the guns
of the cruisers were unmuzzled . . .

Good old Tuppy! I wonder whatever became of him. The
war (which historians remember as "the last gentleman's war"
compared to the kind we have today) was certainly not all
"beer and skittles," to put it politely, but if you don't care a fig
for what's polite and what's not polite in describing it, you can
read what went on in Siegfried Sassoon's terrible account of it,
in *Memoirs of an Infantry Officer,* or in Magnus Hirschfeld's
Sexual History of the World War, an uninhibited account of
one phase of it that gets so worked up (for a medical book) over

Avenue of the Allies — Victory Parade on 5th Avenue, New York (1919).
Painting by Childe Hassam (New York Public Library — Picture Collection)

The Victory Parade, New York (1919) New York's own 27th Division and the Triumphal Arch built specially for them. (New York Public Library — Picture Collection)

what went on in this "last gentleman's war" that the author begs the reader's pardon and asks to be excused for not reporting the awful goings-on in more explicit detail. Thus was the world made safe for democracy by the Allies, despite the shelling, trench rats, typhus, phosgene gas and all the rest. All things considered, Tuppy came through pretty well, except ior the nasty memories.

As a result, he said, his favorite summing up of what went on in 1914-1918 was the line that brought down the curtain in Frederick Lonsdale's acid comedy, *Aren't We All?*, that regaled London and New York in the early Twenties—when someone asks Cyril Maude, the star, "Aren't we all *what?*" — and he explodes with, "Damned fools!"

That's what we were then but to what degree we were to learn the hard way, later, during 1940-45.

New Yorkers who passed through the era immediately following the Great War, as it was called, will remember Maillard's, Huyler's, Schrafft's, Dean's, Ovington's on Fifth Avenue, John Wanamaker, Aeolian and Steinway Halls, Gray's Drug Store (where cut-rate theatre tickets were available up till curtain time), Abdullah cigarettes, fat, oval and gold-tipped (not to mention Fatima, Rameses and Melachrino cigarettes, Sweet Caporal, Hellmar's, Egyptian Deities, etc.) but no one said a word about the dangers of smoking. Men wore spats and sported canes (I wore white linen suits in the summer and white felt hats and smoked long thin cigars), people sailed on the Leviathan, Majestic and the Berengaria and drove Dusenbergs, Pierce Arrows, Packards and Stutz cars, Neysa McMein and Nell Brinkley illustrated Hearst's Sunday supplement with the prettiest girls imaginable, a subject to which Howard Chandler Christy also lent his voluptuous talents, and John Held, Jr. documented it all with his flappers and their boy-friends, the "Sheiks," while the national anthem of the country was not so much "The Star Spangled Banner" anymore but "The Sheik of Araby" (". . . *at night you come to me/Into my tent you creep/At night while I'm asleep . . .*"); or Lupe Velez' recording of "Ma Curly Headed Baby," a lullaby in which the mother asks her babe, "Do you want the moon to play with?" Eh, what about that? That's the kind of time it was . . . . O.O. McIntyre's was the newspaper column everybody read, and Theodore Dreiser, James Branch Cabell, Willa Cather, Sherwood Anderson and Sinclair Lewis were

Times Square (1930) (New York Public Library — Picture Collection)

among the leading novelists, The American Mercury flourish-
ed, following The Smart Set, brain-children of Mencken and
Nathan who also collaborated on a play, *Heliogabalus*, a satire
on "high-jinks" and the like in ancient Rome, with the spiffed
emperor hiccuping lines like "Love is the delusion that one
woman differs from another" or that "Love is the triumph of
the imagination over the intelligence." Jean-Jacques Brousson
came out with his *Anatole France en Pantouffles* and Paul
Morand with his acerbic sketches of post-war Europe — *Open
All night, Green Shoots* (which boasted a foreword by Marcel
Proust) *Closed All Night* and *Lewis and Irene*, William Ger-
hardi's *The Polyglots*, while everyone was reading *The Magic
Mountain* and impecunious poets slept with a copy of Romain
Rolland's *Jean Christophe* as their pillow. *Sex and Character*
by Otto Weininger was the sex book of the day; we read it with
the avidity with which people today read Kinsey and the Hite
and Redbook reports on female sexuality.

I also planned a book at the time, a mystery to be called *Dia-
mond Cut Diamond*, but didn't get beyond the title. Having
heard that the popular magazine, *The Saturday Evening Post*,
paid well for fiction, I studied several of the Clarence Bud-
ington Kelland stories and then, patterning one of my own
after his (he being a very successful contributor to the *Post*), I
sent it in. I had the prettiest of heroines, especially as she ap-
peared in a bathing suit (to inspire the illustrator), the swar-
thiest and most sun-bronzed of tawny-haired heroes to escort
her to all the chic places in a high-powered Hispano Suiza, in
short — the "works." In a few weeks I got it back with an accom-
panying letter to the effect that the editors enjoyed it hugely as
a parody of a typical *Saturday Evening Post* story but it was just
for that reason that they couldn't use it. And nobody worried
about the "Florian Slappey" stories of Octavus Roy Cohn in
the *Post*, about the cullu'd folks being cast in "racist" roles,
ethnic parodies or the like. We had a much lower boiling point
then. Downtown, in Greenwhich Village, Max Gordon lorded
it over The Village Vanguard, the little night club where The
Revuers (Judy Holliday, Betty Comden and Adolph Green)
were first to be seen, and uptown Ed Sullivan, Joe Balaber and
Jean Dubarry ran (if that's the word for what they did there)
the 55th St. Playhouse, a respectable movie "art" house, then,
specializing in foreign films. I was at the Vanguard one late

afternoon when Joe Gould shuffled in with his ubiquitous briefcase which carried the manuscript of his "Oral History of the World." "Max," he said, "either you give me something to eat or I'll throw a fit right in the middle of your dance floor." Soon Max had him chomping away at the specialty of the house that day. John Rose Gildea, Max Bodenheim (New York's own Verlaine, with whom I shared the floor on one of Henry Harrison's poetry readings at the Green Witch Inn, one night), Eli Siegel and his "Hot Afternoons Have Been in Montana," and Harrison with his Greenwich Village Quill, for which I covered the new films, and his slim volume of verse, *Myself Limited,* which had the true Village poet's moan of the day:

> You are the consummation of a dream.
> Tiptoeing to my haunted bed each night.
> Your hands that once caressed me in my dreams
> Are now realities. And lips I kissed
> Innumerable times are phantom lips
> No longer. Dreams are scattered leaves, they say,
> Gathering in a thick heap at the end
> Of years drawn out like secrets from a ghost.
> Of all the tender things that I might say
> Of you, I say this one and only thing:
> You are the consummation of a dream.

or

> What greater sorrow can there be than this:
> To find that love has gone the way of leaves
> Swept by an Autumn wind too tired of beauty?
> Love is minute in grim comparison
> To that which follows love. Who knows the wake
> Of all-consuming passion knows the pain
> Alike no other pain. Sometimes I think
> It wiser far to watch beside a corpse
> Than bury it, and then try to forget.
> What subtler agony than letting love
> Deliberately stab your heart, and stab
> And stab again, the blood refusing to
> Spurt out, gathering in a clot that burns

Like steel inside a crucible? Dear heart,
What greater sorrow can there be than this:
To find that love has gone the way of leaves
Swept by an Autumn wind too tired of beauty?

But for me, the best poem in the book was Harrison's bitter
Fable for Foxes:

Now are the young grapes firm to the vine.
Let the warm wind rush down from the mountain,
Still will the grapes be firm to the vine.
Back will the cool wind lag to the mountain.

Up from the valley the gay fox comes,
Lapping the wind with a sly, quick tongue.
Only for the fine, young grapes he comes—
Prematurely now. But O! how his tongue

Snaps with a hunger for curved, young grapes.
Out of the valley, and now he is there,
Eager to nip the ripening grapes
Firm to the vine too high in the air;

But the gay fox crouches, and leaps with the wind,
Only to snatch a breath of the grapes
Enticing and sly as a twilight wind.
Again the fox leaps for the quivering grapes,

Snapping his teeth on the vine-bound air—
And the earth grows bitter with every fall.
But the ripening grapes are wavering there,
And the fox will clip them, or not at all.

Again and again the mad fox tries—
Longer his tongue, and shorter his breath—
With a cluster of grapes still in his eyes,
And an angry passion now in his breath.

Back to the valley the mad fox goes,
Hotter than the wind that follows him down;
And this furious, smart fox knows:
The well-ripe grapes will never slip down!

But the grapes lie now on the bitter, black earth,
Eager and ready for the valley-bound fox.
But the shy grapes now must rot on the earth,
Yearning for a gay, too impetuous fox.

If only young grapes knew patience a vice!
If only a fox knew patience a virtue!

Samuel Roth, who pirated Joyce's *Ulysses* in his *Two Worlds Monthly* magazine (he also published *Beau,* a very chic literary periodical, and *Two World's Quarterly, Casanova Jr.'s Tales,* etc.) flourished in those halcyon days and ran a Village bookshop, specializing in erotica, but the high class kind, which reminds me again of the 55th St. Playhouse, one of the first of the little cinema "art theatres" of the period with which I was associated. A more corrupt looking trio to be put in charge of running an "art" movie house could hardly be imagined . . . . Ed Sullivan, tall, slim but dubious looking, and with a clipped Noel Coward-like British accent—Joe Balaber, who went around with a "hang-dog" look, if that's how to describe him, anyway, as if "something was eating him," and Jean Dubarry, a little runt with a face that was half what one might imagine the Marquis de Sade looked like if one never saw a picture of de Sade and the other half that of a juvenile delinquent, with a smirk teetering on the edge of whatever he had to say, so that even if he said he was going out for a coffee he looked like he was saying he was going out to some rosy assignation—and that brings in Ilse and Billie Hofmann, a pair of recently-arrived-to-these-shores German hotsy-totsies, hangers on at the theatre when Martin Lewis was managing it (and I was its publicity director), one of whom (Ilse) soon became the girl-friend, if I may put it that way, of the illustrator, James Montgomery Flagg, and the other (Billie) who seemed to be just about everybody's girl. It was the one subject that seemed to be on everybody's mind all the time to such an extent that Ed Sullivan, noticing the perpetual look of deep frustration on the face of Balaber, said to him one afternoon, "Jesus Christ, Joe," he said, "You've been moping around here with that depressing look for months now—I know what you've got staring you in the face all day—I sympathize with you—but what else are you doing here? What are we paying you for?" I never found that out either. (Obviously, this anecdote is cleaned up or I wouldn't have remembered it this long.)

But we showed good pictures, premieres of the new French, German and Russian films, accompanied in the silent-film days by a fellow playing the organ. Friederich Feher, who played the older of the two friends in *The Cabinet of Dr. Caligari*, came in one day and not finding anyone of the staff around began chasing our red-headed French secretary around her desk up in the office until she ran downstairs to the box office for help crying, *"Au secours, au secours!"*

Considering that I started out to be a concert violinist, music played an important part in my life, even though I was "side tracked" from it into the movies in 1927, but in one way or another I kept at it through the years, writing about it, (like the Herald-Tribune articles for Dick Watts' Sunday movie page that started me off in films professionally), scoring silent films, composing, but especially concert-going. I remember a Heifetz performance one night at the Lewisohn Stadium when it began to rain just after his entrance in the Brahms Concerto. Hardly anyone in the audience moved. Nor did he stop playing. Both he and the orchestra carried on valiantly till the end of the first movement. There was an ovation when he turned his fiddle over, as if he were shaking the water out through the "f" holes of his instrument. By this time the rain had let up. He said to the audience, with his usual dead pan, the audience which had remained *en masse* steadfast in their seats, though somewhat huddled together under an occasional umbrella, "If you can stand it, I can." He proceeded to tune up and the second movement began with a renewed drizzle. At the conclusion, there was such an ovation as I had never heard before or since nor must there ever have been a more effulgent evocation of the glorious Brahms' fiddle *Konzertstuck* than as played by him that rainy evening. Another memorable night at the Lewisohn Stadium was the night George Gershwin played the solo part of his *Rhapsody in Blue* and at the moment when the slow movement starts, that melody that became so famous, part of the audience joined in, with the piano and orchestra, humming the tune—a swell of voices that swept across the field and spiralled into the night sky. But after a brief development, the melody repeats itself *forte* and this time the entire audience, the whole 17,000 of them, emboldened now, burst out with it, singing along with the Philharmonic and Gershwin at the piano like a great wave breaking across the strand—a moment's hesitant eddying before the woosh of musical roman candles lit up the night sky and the soloist and orchestra were off on their rocket to the moon . . . . Well, I must say, it was something to have been there that night and it must have done Gershwin's heart good to hear that. (Years later another such incident occurred when, just as Pope John Paul was about to leave the balcony after addressing the crowd gathered to hear him in Mexico City, a burst of young voices began singing Schiller's "Ode to Joy" from Beethoven's *Ninth Symphony,* sweeping across the atrium in front of the Basilica. As the chorus grew louder and louder with others joining in, John Paul turned away from his advisors, went back to the microphone, and in a strong, emotion filled voice, sang with the youth of Mexico.) The night I first heard Ravel's *La Valse* via Mengleberg and the New York Philharmonic, the night I first heard Selim Palmgren's *May Night,* the night I first heard the murmuring cascades of Debussy, and the night I first heard Elman play his own arrangement of Grieg's Nocturne, Op. 54, No. 4, were nights among a thousand and one nights of music I shall never forget. Being a fiddler myself, I was especially taken with everything Heifetz played, did or said. I noted most especially the way he came out on the stage at Carnegie Hall, from the wings through that door on the left—swiftly, like a ship's prow cutting the waves . . . . sometimes even appearing to be finishing a conversation with his accompanist following him, with the ubiquitous page-turner bringing up the rear . . . . But these are just a handful of fragments of memories, snatched here and there from enough I have to fill a book all by themselves. Fittingly enough, I gave up the fiddle—or maybe it gave *me* up—at the end of the Twenties. Doubtless it was for the same reason that Einstein gave it up. When a lady told him it was too bad that he gave it up, he replied, "Ah, no. It would have been too bad if I went on." The violin is an adorable but cruel instrument and nothing shows you up more than when you cannot achieve with it what you want to achieve.

In the Spring of 1929 I made a trip on the Ward Line steamer, *Orizaba,* to Havana. Machado was dictator of Cuba then and no more popular than his successor Batista was to be. Among the tricks that kept him in office was his revocation of the censorship laws everytime the enraged populace began to march in high dudgeon on the presidential palace, whereupon they rushed instead into the theatres and movie houses where now "anything went." When the populace simmered down, the censorship laws were reinstated (ironically, the censorship laws were very strict when they were in force)—to be revoked again the next time Machado became too much for them to stomach. And so on—just like the plot of an operetta. It was all what we used to call "bananas"—no wonder the Latin American countries were known as "banana republics," though they exported bananas too.

Business cards given out by business men are white and have a snap to them. The one Josefina (who worked in a place along the Malecon) gave me was soft and a powder blue. It was really Violeta's card but Josefina had run out of hers and had written her name across it. I was very touched and kept the card for a long time. (But that's the only way I was touched, *grace à Dieu*—and *grace à Josefina, bien sur*.)

There was a lot more to the kind of cockaigne Havana was under the reign (if that's the word for it) of Machado. If you're curious, read Helen Lawrenson's slue-footed *Whistling Girl*—she was there then, too, and didn't miss a beat.

Well, of course the Twenties were more than even Havana under Machado (and I mean it just that way), a lot more, as everyone knows or must have heard, but if I don't get off this very blithe subject I'll never get on with the rest of the book. One could do (and there have been some two dozen such) entire books just on the Twenties and only by reading them all and savoring their illustrations can you begin (and even then *only begin*) to have an idea what this rapturous decade was like . . . . despite the spiritual jitters that earned for the Twenties the sobriquet of "the jazz age." The girls (the "shebas") bobbed their hair and their boy-friends (the "sheiks," after Rudolph Valentino) pomaded theirs, the girls rolled their stockings and the boys wore bell-bottomed trousers, the Charleston was the dance-craze and between dances they "necked" ("Anyone who says they necked," said Groucho Marx, "didn't know his anatomy") and shared the boy's hip flasks of bootleg gin, prohibition still making every swig an illegal one. "Ah," sighed Alexander Woollcott about the ironies of life, since all its pleasures were either "immoral, illegal or fattening," as he put it. Still, what theatre we had! *What Price Glory, Journey's End, Anna Christie, The Front Page* . . . . what films—*The Big Parade* and *The Merry Widow*, Vidor's and Stroheim's, both with Jack Gilbert (and if you didn't see them in New York, then, accompanied by the special musical scores arranged for them by David Mendoza and Billy Axt and played by a full orchestra, then you never really saw them in their pristine state) . . . . and *Variety* and *The Last Laugh* from Ufa, *Potemkin* from the new Soviet republic, the first showing here of which took place on her bed-sheet as a screen in Gloria Swanson's apartment in the Park Chambers Hotel before Symon Gould, Dick Watts, Mal St. Clair, Gloria and Quinn Martin among others, *The Grand Duchess and the Waiter* (by Mal St. Clair, our home-grown Lubitsch, bless him), *Moana* (of course!) and the inimitable Lubitsch himself, while the fronds of low hanging willow tree branches, their leaves brushing the camera's lens as the boat carrying the lovers, Jack Gilbert and Eleanor Boardman, gliding along the banks of the stream (in Vidor's *Bardleys the Magnificent*) . . . . the leaves literally kissing the camera's lens . . . . That's the kind of cinema we once had in place of the swill we now have to put up with (I don't mean you, dar-lings, *Slave of Love*, *Peppermint Soda*, and *Days of Heaven*. Good old King Vidor . . . . !)

It was a time . . . . !

. . .

In the Spring of '79, I made some revisions on this book, some deletions, some amendments, among the latter being an excerpt from a letter (which I append here) from Liam O'Leary of Dublin, an Irish film poet who had done a book (the only one extant) on another Irish film poet, Rex Ingram (*The Four Horsemen of the Apocalypse, Mare Nostrum,* the first *Garden of Allah,* etc.) which currently languishes for want of a publisher,* who closed his letter to me saying "Saw Resnais' *Providence* which I loathed. I'm beginning to think that the only humanity left to the screen will be in porn films. I'm becoming so disappointed with the films I see. Thank God for Claude Goretta (*The Lace Maker, Invitation*). This is not a great age. How grateful we should be to have lived through the Twenties."

*He has since found a publisher—and in Dublin, too.

"The first love, the first sunrise, the first South Sea Island, are memories apart."

— Robert Louis Stevenson

(She)

"Oh, what you say is awful! But the feeling that is
called love does exist among people, and is given
not for months or years, but for a lifetime!"

(He)

"No, it does not! Even if we should grant that a
man might prefer a certain woman all his life, the
woman in all probability would prefer someone
else; and so it has always been and still is in the
world," he said . . .

"But the feeling may be reciprocal," said the
lawyer.

"No, sir, it can't!" rejoined the other. "Just as it
cannot be that in a cartload of peas, two marked
peas will lie side by side . . . To love one person
for a whole lifetime is like saying that one candle
will burn a whole lifetime . . ."

— TOLSTOY

Kreutzer Sonata

OLD SONGS — OLD LOVES

ERNA (1929-1936)

It was to be just for six weeks. "Go down, staff it, get it ready
— we'll do the booking from up here — and you can come
back in six weeks," they said. They owned the 55th St. Play-
house in New York and had just acquired the Little Theatre in
Baltimore. I was on the staff of the 55th St. Playhouse. "All
right," I said, "but remember, not a second more than six
weeks." The time was the late Fall of 1929. The giddy Twenties
were coming to an end, but we were all still going on the past
momentum of those blithe years.

November — and I was there, Baltimore, a quiet, even
sleepy, Southern town, south of the Civil War Mason & Dixon
Line and pro-Confederate during that parlous time. Standing
on the corner of Howard & Franklin streets I wondered what
this place, so different from New York, would have in store for
me, but it was only six weeks, I remembered, what did it mat-
ter? I took lunch in the Congress Hotel nearby, and later
checked into the Knights of Columbus Club. That afternoon I
called in an ad to the local Sun paper. "Wanted: Four attrac-
tive girls as ushers. Apply Little Theatre, 523 N. Howard St.

between 10 a.m. and 12 noon Friday."

Friday at 10 a.m. I was there and they began streaming in — perhaps a dozen of them. I picked four and was about to leave for lunch when a girl came running up the stairs into the office (it was already past twelve) wondering if she was too late. "Yes, I said. "I just engaged four girls. That's all I need."

I said this mechanically, as I would have said to anyone applying for the job at that moment — only this wasn't "anyone." "My god!" I thought, as I looked at the apparition before me, for she was the prettiest little witch I ever did see. [A cat, when it eyes a place to where it wants to spring, measures it with its eyes and then springs, landing just where it wants to land, having known exactly the velocity required. In his autobiography, Chaplin put it quite simply when he said ". . . every man, whether he be young or old, when meeting any woman, measures the potentiality of sex between them. Thus it has always been with me." And me. (Not you?)] "What's the matter with you?" said my demon spirit, jabbing me with his pitchfork. "You goin' blind all of a sudden?" As she smiled and turned to go, I stammered, "Look, you'd better give me your name, address and telephone, just in case one of the others doesn't show up — or whatever." Whatever, indeed! I don't even remember what I told the fourth one I'd engaged, when she had shown up, poor girl — all I remember is that my little witch was going to be hired, come hell or high water, as we used to say. (At that moment the water began to rise but I didn't see it — I had eyes only for her.) "Loved anyone who loved not at first sight?" — like the poet said. Her name was Erna and she came from Latvia, I was to discover, and she spoke German and an English with the faintest and for me the most irresistible of accents. The prettiest girls, I decided then and there, obviously came from the North of Europe — the Baltic — Sweden (Garbo), North Germany (Dietrich), Latvia (Erna) — and Erna appeared to be a combination of the two. What a combination!

You wouldn't think a casual thing like that — giving a girl a job — could change the course of your life, would you? But it changed mine, turning the six weeks I was going to stay there to six years. She not only got the job as usherette but was soon promoted to cashier, so she wouldn't have to stand.

Our first date was as idyllic as it could be—on a moonlit autumn night— the moon, that old procuress—in a park by a pond.

Such a night as a Chinese poet (Lin Pu, tenth century) once described when he sought to evoke a night of the purest enchantment with:

> *Blue water . . . clear moon . . .*
> *In the moonlight white herons*
>   *are flying . . .*
> *Listen! Do you hear the girls who*
>   *gather water chestnuts?*
> *They are going home in the night,*
>   *singing.*

As you can see, I was, as Yeats put it, "looped in the loop of her hair" — Through a realm of mosses, lichens and flowering blackthorne we trod, holding hands, through paths bordered by wood sorrel, iris and larkspur. We sat on a rock jutting out into the pond because I'd heard on such eves frogs would sometimes pop out and croak their little songs. I'd never seen a frog. We sat, hardly saying a word (some other couples were there too) waiting for the frogs to come out. They came and we exchanged silent smiles and — here let Joyce describe what happened as he once did so incomparably with:

> *Along with us, the summer wind*
> *Went murmuring — O happily! —*
> *But softer than the breath of summer*
> *Was the kiss she gave to me.*

"Every man who goes in pursuit of game," wrote Nelson Bryant, sports editor of The New York Times years later, "is also after a unicorn of his own devising." In this, the unicorn for me was to be my first love, but I didn't realize it at the time. For me it was a fragrant autumn night in which that year's "Indian Summer" still lingered. For Bryant it was autumn, too, at dusk . . . "dull, dark and soundless" . . . as Poe would have described it, ". . . when the clouds hung oppressively low in the heavens . . ."

". . . I walked past gnarled and neglected apple trees," Bryant wrote, "their bare arms twisting against dark clouds . . . and I imagined them ripe with pomegranates while underfoot wild strawberries were ready for eating . . . At the marsh the ducks were flying but they were far out of range and later dark masses of clouds in the west were mountains against the crimson fading light and it was too late to shoot. I sat and waited for the black ducks to return from the ocean to the marshes, the brooks and ponds. They came, as they always do, when there is so little light remaining, one often hears their wings before their dark forms materialize overhead in the murk. Later, on the way home, a nearly full moon blazed across the fields, and on the edge of the white oak woods, ethereal in that strange, cold light, the white figure of what must have been a unicorn moved and was gone. To try to capture him would have been useless, for no unicorn has ever been taken unless first beguiled by a maiden, and I was alone."

I was more fortunate. I, too, was alone with her the night I found my unicorn, for she was maiden and unicorn, for me in one — each beguiling the other . . . and both beguiling me . . .

I used to call her by the German pet-name of "Puppchen" (little doll) which reminded her of a song that went:

    Puppchen, du bist meine Augenstern . . .

    (Little doll, you are my eye's delight)

She also had, among her few possessions, a small mandolin on which she played a Russian cossack dance — the only piece she knew. Months later she inscribed it to me — that's right, right on the wooden face of the instrument — *Erinnerung an so viele frohliche Stunden* (Memories of so many happy hours). Her only other belongings consisted of her clothes and a picture of her mother. One suitcase held it all.

What must it be like, I thought, to live from salary to salary when that salary was a small one and that's all there was? Like crossing a torrential stream from stone to stone, at the very least?

Making the rounds of what became some of our favorite eating places was a revelation for her and me — especially for her, since eating regularly hadn't been such a regular thing for her — Rossiter's, the Rennert and Southern Hotels, Miller's, and the like, for hard, soft, devilled and steamed crabs, and oysters from Chesapeake Bay* and the Eastern Shore, the Congress Hotel for terrapin, Virginia and Smithfield hams, Hopper McGaw's, that fancy grocer's and delightful snack bar and even a Chinese restaurant, Woh Lee's, which constituted the whole of Baltimore's "Chinatown." Not to mention the Lex-

---

*One need only recall Mencken's dithyramb on Baltimore's "indigenous victualizing that was unsurpassed in the Republic" in *Happy Days*. "Baltimore lay very near the immense protein factory of the Chesapeake Bay and out of it ate divinely."

Erna — before *Autumn Fire* (1930) (Photo by the author)

ington Market (like the fabulous Farmer's Market in Holly-
wood) with its "Arabian Nights" bazaar of gustatory delights to
eat there or to take home.

The only drawback was Prohibition, that nasty trick played
on America's troops returning from France in 1919 only to find
that a law, called the "Volstead Act," had forbidden the con-
sumption of alcoholic liquors. You could get your head blown
off in France during the war but you couldn't get a drink when
you got back. And so the institutions of the speakeasy and the
bootlegger flourished, offering all the liquor you wanted.
"Right off the boat," my bootlegger used to say, whereupon
the usual rejoinder to this stock offering was, "You mean,
scraped right off the side of the boat, eh?" And whatever it was
— whiskey, rum, gin, vodka — it usually tasted that way.
Besides periodic visits from my bootlegger who, when he
opened his great coat which he wore in all weathers, displayed
linings adapted to hold eight bottles, four on each side, I had
periodic visits from a filmlegger, too, whose stock in trade was
"hot films." All the so-called "artistic sexual breakthroughs" on
the screen that you hear touted about today was old stuff back
in the Twenties and Thirties, although we didn't pretend they
were anything else but what they were — dirty films . . . nor
did we imagine that you could see stuff like this publicly and
thereby feel enlightened.

I'd just finished reading Max Brod's novel, *"Die Frau, nach
der man sich sehnt"* (The Woman For Whom One Yearns),
which had been filmed in Germany in 1928 starring Dietrich
and Fritz Kortner and shown here under the title of *Three
Loves*. When Dietrich heard this, she wrote me asking to send
her the American reviews (her first reviews in America — she
had written from a suburb of Berlin, Wilmersdorf, where she
lived, right after the completion of *The Blue Angel*) which I
did — they were very good — and an augury of things to come.

Anyway, I gave Erna the novel to read. It was a highly
romantic tale by Brod (who was to become the literary execu-
tor of Kafka, his dearest friend) about the chance meeting of a
couple — Stasha and Erwin — (just like ours, I told her) — in
which Stasha, with a premonition that fate wouldn't give her a
break so she could find happiness, dies in Erwin's arms in the
film, saying, "I have had three loves and I have lost them all."
She had warned Erwin about herself, saying *"Liebe mich wen-
iger, dann liebst du mich recht."* (Love me less, then you will

love me right.) And Erna would point that passage out to me in the book. From that moment on I would sometimes call her Stasha which, although it would make her smile, didn't keep her from autographing a photograph I took of her with Stasha's admonition to Erwin. I didn't take it seriously . . . her smile on the photograph was very affectionate, that's all that mattered . . . .

She had a talent for drawing and during the long hours sitting in the box office as cashier she would do nudes and portraits (I have reproduced a self-portrait with her autograph: *"Für Dich, mein Lebenslicht — ich hoffe die Flamme soll ewig flackern!"* Stasha, April 29th, 1931) (For you, light of my life — I hope the flame will ever burn brightly! — Stasha)

She also had an odd way of adding figures. In a column of figures she would pick out the numbers that together added up easily, like 5 and 5 or 6 and 4 or 9 and 1, then, having "disposed" of those, she would go back and, gritting her teeth at the prospect, would then proceed to add up the remaining numbers, the while retaining the sum of the first batch of numbers she added in her head, and when she had the sum of the second batch of figures, she would then add the two which would give her the total for that column. It was so bizarre I didn't know what to say when I first watched her add a column of figures, totalling up the number of tickets sold at the end of each day. Years later, when I read in Salinger's *Catcher in the Rye* (which became my favorite of all American novels) of that girl who, when playing checkers, after having all her kings crowned, would keep them in the back row just because she like the way they looked there, I was reminded of the way Erna added. It was just as screwy. Salinger wasn't exaggerating — he knew exactly what he was doing. The exasperating thing about it was that her totals always came out right so that any attempts of mine to wean her away from making things hard for herself fell on deaf ears. She said she was making things *easier* for herself and couldn't understand why I was complaining. "You know," I said to her the first night I witnessed this strange new arithmetic, "if you're going to add like that from now on, maybe you shouldn't be cashier." "You're not going to put me back on the floor again!" she snapped. "No, angel," I said, "but if the New York office ever found out you added like that, you wouldn't last on this job 5 minutes more — no matter how correct it came out. They don't have any imagination in the

Self-Portrait and dedication to the author by Erna. "Fur Dich, mein Lebens-licht — Ich hoffe die Flamme soll ewig flackern . . .!" (For you, light of my life — I hope the flame will ever be lighted) April 29, 1931

New York office — no poetry, no sense of humor." To which she burst out laughing, in which I joined. What else could you do.

If you think *that* odd, what do you suppose she came up with next?

An abacus.

"What's that for?" I asked.

"It's an abacus — you count with it — my brother . . ."

"I know it's an abacus — and you know how to use it?"

"Yes — my brother, he's a sailor, got it in Tonkin and gave it to me."

"And you can count with it?"

"Uhuh — correct and fast — he showed me. Wanna learn? It's easy."

"And you're going to make change and all with that thing — right in front of the patrons?"

A worried look came into her eyes.

"Y'know, you're crazy," I said. "Absolutely nuts. You're going to sit there making change with an abacus while the patron stares at you in amazed disbelief?"

She had picked up the abacus and now held it with both hands close to her. She looked uneasily at me, with no word to say.

"We'll be the laughing-stock of the town — they'll write it up in all the newspapers — you'll get your picture in the papers," I went on. "And if the New York office ever gets wind of it, oh boy, you'll be out of a job so fast (and so will I) it won't be funny — !"

"All right," she said, putting it back in the bag in which she'd brought it, *"All right!"*

"Show me how you do it," I said. I'd never seen anyone manipulate an abacus.

"Give me a problem," she smiled, perking up, the cloud gone from her face, maybe thinking she still had a chance with it . . .

"83 X 5" I said. 83¢ was the evening admission.

She began sliding the little black beads along the wires back and forth, up and down, on the two sides of the counting board so fast that I couldn't follow her movements. All that came through was a succession of clicks — like a typewriter.

"415," she said. "$4.15."

I figured it out with a pencil and she was right.

I smiled.

"Very clever, those Chinese," I said, "but you're not Chinese and this isn't a joss-house and we're not in Tonkin. Now put it away — we're going to have to do it the hard way, I'm afraid. Can you add?"

"Try me," she said.

"One and one," I said.

"Two," she replied, tears welling up in her eyes. I hugged her.

"Right," I said, and she smiled through her tears. "You're going to make a fine cashier!"

Shortly after her two brushes with the mysteries of arithmetic and her way of solving them, I asked her, "Do you do everything screwy?"

She smiled. "Not everything."

She not only stayed on as cashier but after a while was further promoted (if that's the word for it) to become my wife.

Six weeks indeed!

Costumes were ordered for the usherettes and cashiers (we had two, for the day and night shifts), deep blue velveteen pants with scarlet sateen blouses, coffee service for those patrons who would like a demi-tasse, detailed programs (going to the movies had class in those days), tickets, posters for the first program — *Shiraz* — a film from India, telling the legend of the building of the Taj Mahal. Meanwhile, business tycoons who had lost everything in the Wall Street stock market crash between late October (did I forget to say the year was 1929?) and mid-November were throwing themselves out of their office or hotel windows — the lack of more margin being the straw that broke the back of the Big Bull Market and signalled the end of the Coolidge-Hoover prosperity era.

Not only tycoons, everyone who invested in stocks was all but wiped out on that Black Friday in October which marked the beginning of the bottom falling out of the market. Men were selling apples on Fifth Avenue, New York for 5¢ each — soup kitchens were set up in Times Square, breadlines were everywhere, banks were closing one after the other and unemployment was rife as industry all but ground to a halt. The Great Depression rose like the great mushroom cloud fifteen years later that marked the detonating of the atom bomb over Hiroshima — a depression that was to engulf all — except those who escaped it . . . like us.

"On that date, a Tuesday in 1929," Pete Hamill was to say in The New York Daily News of October 29, 1979, "the United States paid for 10 years of greed and stupidity with the greatest financial collapse in history."

Although thousands were financially ruined overnight and the appalling statistics of stock losses turned the period into an economic nightmare . . . we opened the season at the Little with a dreamy film about the great love of a seventeenth century emperor of India, the Shah Jehan, for his favorite wife, Mumtaz Mahal, and how when she died he ordered built for her, out of his grief, a fabulous mausoleum. (Of course, what the film did not tell was *why* she died at the age of 39 — from having been delivered of so many children that she died in childbirth after having been delivered of what was to be her last. And, mind you, she was only *one* of his several wives. And a creep like that goes down in history as an enduring romantic figure and his monument to the victim of his passion immortalized as the most ethereal tribute on earth to a great love!)

The Shahs haven't changed — the years make no difference. In our own time, Shah Reza Pahlevi of Iran, passing on the footage shot by Albert Lamorisse (director of that exquisite little film, *The Red Balloon)* for a documentary film Lamorisse was making across Europe and Asia, shooting from a balloon, rejected the "picturesque" vistas Lamorisse had shot of the relics of ancient Persia and said he wouldn't pass them unless Lamorisse included footage of Iran's modern oil refineries, derricks, power stations, and the like, to show how modern Iran was. Lamorisse went back to shoot this modern stuff, his balloon brushed against one of the charged electric wires, and Lamorisse was killed.

These were still the days of the silent films and we had an electric double turn-table playing 78 rpm records presided over by someone engaged for just that, to watch the cue-sheets and play those records selected to fit specific scenes in the film. I, of course, did the scoring — that was a fine point I wouldn't trust to anyone else. The right music for silent films was as important as later the right dialogue was to be when the sound-film finally arrived. Music took the place of dialogue in the silent film, though actually — when rightly used — it did far more, it "sang along" with the film, which was the point of my three articles in The New York Herald-Tribune, the year before, the articles which catapulted me from music into movies in the first place.

I might characterize the time, the place and the girl (which was the title of an operetta by Victor Herbert, by the way) by saying that the background music for many of the films was often drawn from some then current favorites of mine which, on the rare occasions when I hear them again, still remind me, after all these years, of "the time, the place and the girl" — 1930-33, to wit:

Syncopated Love Song and *A Mood in Blue* by Dana Seuss — *Vanilla Blossoms*, Tango, by Nat Shilkret — Duke Ellington's *Black and Tan* — Werner Janssen's *New Year's Eve in New York. In Days Gone By* from "The Countess Maritza" (Emmerich Kalman) . . .

We followed *Shiraz* with other silent films, chiefly from Europe, mostly from Germany and the Soviet Union. We had the pick of the field, which was our unique position in the town since we were the only "foreign" house. We showed *Die Hose* (The Pants) from the satire by Carl Sternheim about a man (a bourgeois German in a small town) who was made to wear horns by the local Duke and his close advisor and how the horns fit him so well that he showed them off. With Werner Krauss as the German cluck and Jenny Jugo as his toothsome little cookie of a wife, Krauss never had a role which fitted him better. We showed *The Wonderful Lie of Nina Petrovna*, with Brigitte Helm as the mistress of a high officer in the Czar's retinue who falls in love with a penniless young officer (Franz Lederer) and leaves the high officer for the younger man. But when the younger man is caught cheating at cards (to get enough money to support her) the high officer is about to ruin him (he has since found out that he lost his mistress to the younger man) by having him discharged dishonorably from the army, when Nina, hearing of this, to save her young man, returns to the high officer. It is only later that the high officer realizes he has not really won her back at all when he finds her dead, by her own hand, wearing the cheap pair of shoes the young officer had bought her once during their brief few weeks together. This was also a UFA film, from the golden age of the German silent film. But we showed others, too, from France and England, such as Renoir's *Little Match Girl*, Hitchcock's *The Lodger*, from the Belloc-Lowndes novel with which he was to inaugurate the screen genre he made so successfully his own, the suspense-thriller; Dietrich in *Three Loves* (made just before *The Blue Angel*); Russian and German films galore, when Soviet Union, Germany and Hollywood were leading the film world after the First World War. Olga Preobrezhenskaya's *Peasant Women of Riazan* (called *The Village of Sin* here), which Eisenstein would not have hesitated to sign, showed that women as first-rate directors is old stuff in the movies. (Harry Stack Sullivan, no less, the noted psychiatrist, acted as my defense counsel when the Maryland censors tried to ban it.) *Old and New* by Sergei Mikhailovitch himself, bursting with the joy of Russia's new life, Turin's poetic documentary, *Turksib*, on the building of the first railway from Turkestan to Siberia, the Kozintsev-Trauberg *New Babylon*, that sardonic masterpiece on the Paris Commune, as if Delacroix had collaborated with them on it, Pudovkin's *Storm Over Asia*, on the favorite theme of the director of *Mother* and *The End of St. Petersburg*, the awakening to revolutionary consciousness of a simple non-political being (and as Fedya in Tolstoy's *The Living Corpse*, directed by Ozep but with montage by Pudovkin — who else?), Dovzhenko's incredible *Arsenal* and his ecstatic *Earth*, another by the Kozintsev-Trauberg team, *China Express*, which, with *Storm Over Asia*, foretold the coming whirlwind that would kick out the white exploiters and Kuomintang clique from China in the path of Mao Tse Tung's "Long March" and realize the reorganization of China for the Chinese; *Pandora's Box*, after Wedekind and by Pabst, with our own Louise Brooks as Lulu ("Without Brooks, I don't make the picture," Pabst had said and he proved how right he was), Paul Leni's *The Waxworks*, a triptych, with Emil Jannings as the Caliph Haroun-al-Raschid, Conrad Veidt as Ivan the Terrible and Werner Krauss as Jack-the-Ripper — all new films then but which have since become enshrined in the cinema's pantheon.

I would often watch the patrons who came in and sometimes would speak with them. I remember one who dragged himself along on crutches, but whose head was magnificent, the head of a faun if there ever was one in real life. Surely it was one like him whom Mallarmé thought of when he began, "A faun, a simple sensuous being . . ." I introduced myself and spoke to him. His bitter face broke into a wonderful smile. Yes, he liked the films we showed and came as often as he could. No, it was no problem — he came by taxi. What did he do? He painted.

Somehow I never got around to asking him if I could see his work. That was wrong of me, not for politeness' sake, but I was really curious to see what kind of paintings his condition impelled him to do. Now I will never know.

Sometimes Mencken would come in (he lived in Baltimore) and Huntington Cairns, the great classic scholar, then with the Mellon Gallery in Washington; Aaron Sopher, the artist, Richard Pratt of the Enoch Pratt Library. Being a Mencken fan (as who wasn't in those days?), I sent him a press pass to the theatre. He returned it with a letter saying: "Thanks, but as I am already a paying patron of your theatre it would be unfair of me to accept this. I go seldom but when I do I always find something interesting." For relaxation after the show, we would go to the Peabody Book Shop on North Charles Street, which harbored in its rear the Siegfried Stube, named after one of the two proprietors of the shop — Otto and Siegfried Weisberger. In this *Nachtlokal,* a real old time German café, you could get sandwiches, leberwurst, bratwurst, bauernwurst, weisswurst, knockwurst, the whole melodious repertoire, and beer, the while being regaled by a violinist and pianist playing old Viennese waltzes and sentimental German songs. There was a bust of Shakespeare on the piano with a man's fedora placed cockily over his brow. It reminded me of the marble Virgin of the Cathedral of Chartres where, on the new high altar, she was decked out with the Phrygian cap of Liberty during the French Revolution, "à la Marianne" of Daumier. It was here, at the first table as you entered, that you would invariably find Ludwig Teach, surely one of that era's adornments of the human race, and his constant companion, his little dachshund, Waldi. Both would be nursing a beer, interrupted by relightings of Ludwig's pipe. I was to remain his friend throughout the years that followed until we were separated by You-Know-Who — *Hamavdil* — "The Great Divider." Teach was proof, as much as anyone else ever was proof, of the truth of Nietzsche's adage that life would be a mistake without music. (I think of the voluminous Nietzsche-Wagner correspondence — but you should see the letters *I* got from Teach — several hundred of them — they are something to read!) He was the founder and guiding spirit of the Bach Club which sponsored periodic concerts (by the Compinsky Trio, the pianist Vilma Kaplan, etc.) and it was sometimes at this home on East Madison Street, where he used to play his favorite com-

Huntington Cairns (1930) (Photo: Aycock Brown) (Courtesy of H. Cairns)

poser, Brahms,* on the piano after dinner (the *Intermezzi*, which he especially liked), that I was permitted to be present at soirées of the Saturday Night Club when Mencken (at the piano) and the other nine (mostly strings, but also a French horn and double-bass, as I recall) recruited chiefly from Mencken's medical friends, would gather from time to time on weekends to play chamber music — Haydn, Schubert, Beethoven. The Club had for its coat of arms four quarters on a shield consisting of a fiddle and bow crossed, as they used to cross rapiers over a fireplace, a large and succulent looking lobster, pretzels and onions, and, of course, a seidel of foaming beer (surely meant to be Wurzburger or Loewenbrau). It was at Teach's that I met Huntington Cairns, that Thoreau of the Outer Banks of North Carolina, classical scholar (with Edith Hamilton he edited all of Plato) and a remarkable volume that defined the limits of art in literature. And it was at Teach's that I also met Dr. Dandy, one of the great brain surgeons of the time.

Siegfried Weisberger was a wild-eyed, bushy mustached chap who looked like Nietzsche and who, I'm sure, would have given the author of "Thus Spake Zarathustra" a hard time. "What d' you mean: 'The distance between the ape and man is not so great as the distance between Man and the Superman.'? You can stir up a lot of trouble talking like that!" In what other bookshop's bargain table could one find, as I did on the way into the stube one night, an illustrated copy of Magnus Hirschfeld's "Sexual History of the World War"? But he was one of the most genial (as well as learned, his hobby being music) fellows I ever met.

And while I am on the subject of friends of those great days, I must mention V. F. Calverton, sociologist and sexologist, as well as editor-publisher of first The Modern Quarterly, then The Modern Monthly; Eli Siegel, the poet, who used to declaim during midnight walks from Vachel Lindsay's hair-raising "The Congo" or his own lyrical "Hot Afternoons Have Been in Montana" which won The Nation Poetry Award in 1925 . . .

---

*He gave me a copy of a rare photograph he had of Brahms in a "*katzenjammer*" mood, playing the gay Lothario with his fetching housemaid. I have reproduced it here.

Ludwig Teach and Waldi (1930) (Courtesy of Janet Teach)

Johannes Brahms (Courtesy of Ludwig Teach) A rare candid photo of Johannes Brahms, given to the author by Teach. (Brahms was his favorite composer) (Collection of the author)

> *Quiet and green was the grass in the*
> *field,*
> *The sky was whole in brightness,*
> *And O, a bird was flying, high, there*
> *in the sky,*
> *So gently, so carelessly and fairly . . .*

Jo Hurwitz, who would declaim with equal lyric passion from Dowson,

> *Last night, ah, yesternight, betwixt*
> *her lips and mine*
> *There fell thy shadow, Cynara! thy*
> *breath was shed*
> *Upon my soul between the kisses and*
> *the wine . . .*

The black and white line artist, Aaron Sopher, whose pen was as acid as that of Georg Grosz; the dermatologist, Mark Hollander, who used to deliver all forty (or was it more?) stanzas of that heart-rending epic of the Old West, "The Ballad of Kansas Lil", with its numbing end —

> *Lil died with her boots on*
> *Where she fell,*
> *So what the hell, boys,*
> *What the hell!*

Nor must I fail to mention Donald Kirkley, The Sun's movie critic, who was equally adept at giving out with (I'm sure it must have been) all ninety stanzas of another famous ballad (attributed by all and sundry to no less than Rudyard Kipling) that started out —

> *O the minstrels sing of an English king*
> *Of a thousand years ago,*
> *Who ruled his land with an iron hand,*
> *But his mind was weak and low.*
> *He was hairy and wooly and full of fleas,*
> *His terrible tool hung down to his knees,*
> *The son of a bitch, the bastard King of*
> *England!*
> *Now the Queen of France . . .*

. . . and so on . . . until the whole hierarchy of Europe's royalty was involved, as improperly as could be.

Which would seem to be the proper place for me to take note of an improper visit I paid one night on the recommendation — what recommendation? nay, urging! — of friends to see

Siegfried Weisberger and Teach (1930) "*You see? I told you it was F Sharp* . . ." (Courtesy of Janet Teach)

a young new Polish stripper at a burlesque house on what must
be, or was then, one of the seediest and most disreputable
quarters on the East Coast — East Baltimore Street. The thing
about Hinda Wassau (I wonder what ever became of her) was
that she took off where other strippers finished. She was, in
fact, "the Heifetz of the strippers," coming out already nude
and beginning her act from there. And if you can't imagine
what she could possibly do from that point on, it's not that you
haven't a free-wheeling imagination, it's just that you have
never seen Miss Wassau doing her thing. An institution like she
was should have been subsidized. And speaking of free-
wheeling, this was the time when the Republic, a Minsky bur-
lesque house, flourished on 42nd St., just west of Seventh Ave-
nue in New York. Each week there was a change of its electric-
lights sign advertising its featured attraction, in which fa-
cetiousness was raised to new heights (or would it be "lowered
to new depths"?). One week, for instance, the star attraction
was billed as "Fannie Hurts from Wheeling." That'll give you
an idea of the lovely innocence of burlesque in those days. Or
the act in which two bums are on the stage watching a pretty
girl sashay by. Across the stage, she stops and bends over to ad-
just her garter while one of the bums takes out a pair of binocu-
lars and begins to focus on her. The other bum, who apparent-
ly has never even seen binoculars, stares bewildered at his
friend and asks him, "What are you doing?" "I'm scrutinizing
her," his learned friend replies, the binocs still fixed on her as
she still bends over fixing her garter. "All the way from *there*?"
asks the other bum, incredulously, as he waves his hand be-
tween his friend at one end of the stage and the girl bending
over at the other end. He doesn't encounter anything and
shakes his head, puzzled. I mean, that was the charm of bur-
lesque in those days. And vaudeville — anywhere, but especial-
ly at the mecca of all vaudevillians, the Palace, that two-a-day,
reserved seat, two-dollars-top Taj Mahal of variety acts, where
such as George Givot, Tom Howard and Jimmy Durante were
to be seen, if you were lucky enough to have tickets. And the
Marx Brothers, Clark & McCullough, Jimmy Savo, W.C.
Fields and all the rest. George Givot, "The Greek Ambassador
of Good Will," as he was billed, who delivered a monologue
that would have delighted James Joyce with its playing with the
English language via syllogisms, puns and other settings of the
language on its ear, such as his references to scientists as

"sciencestiffs" and debutantes as "debutramps" etc. Or
Tom Howard's triste monologue on the difficulties of life on
the farm, his father's farm, where his father paid him only a
quarter a week. "I can't live on a quarter a week," he said,
then, after a pause, "not the way *I* live." Or Jimmy Durante's
homily about money. "What good is it?" he asks. "It can't buy
the things that really matter if you don't have them — good
health, the love of your family, the loyalty of your friends,
through thick and thin, and so on . . ." He walks off stage,
sadly shaking his head, but just before disappearing off stage
he stops, looks up and grins, "Of course, I been talkin' about
Confederate money!"

It was the age of innocence and it was a lovely age. Things
had weights, balances and measures, in relation to each other
— not like the chaos existing today. You knew where you were
in relation to all the things you encountered — in what Gilbert
Seldes called "the lively arts" and all the rest.

Finally, there was the quartet at Dick Murphy's, around the
corner from the Little Theatre, on Franklin Street, where there
was a piano — an old Bechstein, which made Dick's place a
mecca for me. Nights after the show, when Dick, his wife
Ruth, the two painters — Luke Morgoreth and Karl Metzler
(both of whom did portraits of me) — and Angelo Bisenz, a
vast spaghetti eater, voluptuary and would-be aesthete à la
Swinburne —

> *Cold eyelids that hide like a jewel*
> (he would intone to Erna across the table)
> *Hard eyes that grow soft for an hour,*
> *The heavy white limbs and the cruel red*
>   *mouth*
> *Like a venomous flower —*
> *Dolores, my lady of pain . . .**
> (then, without the slightest pause)

"What are you doing after the show?"

"You're too late," I said, "I already asked her that." Which
gave him the hiccups, whereupon everyone proceeded to try to
help him by slapping him on the back. Everyone except Erna.
She remained seated and chided him, "I told you not to drink
so much."

He turned to her testily and through half-closed eyes said,

*Swinburne, quoted by Lee Gentry (Claude Raines) to his lady fair in Ben
Hecht's *Crime Without Passion*.

A party at the home of Peter Lorre in Hollywood celebrating the arrival there of G.W. Pabst. On the couch, L. to R. — Pabst, Fritz Lang, Peter Lorre, Erich von Stroheim. Hovering over the couch is Joseph ("Pepe") Schildkraut. (1984) (Collection of the author) (Courtesy of "Filmkunst", Vienna.)

"It's my way to avoid the miseries of a hangover."

"How so?" asked Dick.

"By staying drunk," he said.

We would gather for a late spaghetti supper, I would be at the piano. Eventually a Nocturne emerged from my ramblings over the keys, completed during a cruise on the old Dutch liner, *Rotterdam*, in 1936.

When seated at table, Dick would deliver a homily such as one from the good Dr. Johnson I remember, "A man is in general better pleased when he has a good dinner on the table than if his wife can speak Greek." Whereupon Dick turned to his wife, saying "You can't speak Greek, can you?" To which she replied, *"Thalatta! Thalatta!"* "You see?" he said, " 'The Sea! . . . The Sea!' It's from some Greek play. That's all she knows." Then, to her — "You don't know anymore Greek than that, I hope?" "I should say not!" she replied. *"Bon appétit,"* said Dick to us, and we dug in. I recall now a similar remark made years later by Ernest Boyd at a midnight repast in the Barberry Room in New York when he told Tom Curtiss, Stroheim, Denise Vernac and me that women needed only to be charming and to see that the seams of their stockings were straight. Since he was the American translator of de Maupassant we forgave him his facetiousness. He also didn't recognize the existence of aeroplanes. That was all right with me, as neither did I.

By this time I had sent for my family, having decided that I was going to stay on and they might as well be here, too. Mom and dad came, and my two brothers, one of whom, Max, became my assistant at the theatre. The other, Arthur, studied law and from that went into theatrics, under the name of Eric Arthur.

Erna being on the night shift as cashier in the theatre sat selling tickets while I would lie on the shelf below her, unseen by those who came to the box office to buy tickets, and would keep her company, talking to her, joking . . . It was then I got the idea to make a film with her, which was to be my "trump card." (The only card game I ever played was blackjack, or twenty-one — in which you can lose a lot of money much faster than in poker and I was flatly no good at it so, "unlucky in cards, lucky in love," I said to myself and proceeded to woo this damsel whom I had "netted." My daughter tells me I am invariably years behind in my use of slang but if they don't say "woo" anymore, as they probably don't, it's too bad, as it was a pretty word.)

The film was to do it, which was much to ask of any film, considering the prize. I told her I was thinking of buying a motion-picture camera and wanted to try it out. Would she pose for me? Sure — why not? We would go off together on weekends (Sundays) and I would shoot away, in the woods, by a house, across a field or stream, on a train to Washington, by a railway station, etc. One day a young man came to the theatre selling vacuum cleaners. I said I didn't need a vacuum cleaner and besides I already had one. "That's what they all say," he said. "They all have one." A pause. "How would you like to be in the movies?" I said. "I thought that was only said to girls," he said. "No, I'm serious, I'm shooting a film and I need a young man and you'll do." "Well" he said, "It's the best offer I've had today . . ."

It was settled — he was to be my leading man. His name was Willy Hildebrand. He and Erna never met. She, of course, never knew she was appearing in a film that had a story (of sorts, about a boy and girl who were once in love, had fallen out of love, and who fell back again in love — paralleled with the change of the seasons, from autumn through winter to spring). Shooting took almost a year and in June of '31 (we began the film in the early Fall of '30) I asked her if she'd like to see the film she starred in. "I *starred* in a film?" she asked. "What are you talking about?" I told her. "Oh, that one . . . the one you were testing the camera . . .?" There was a pause. Then quietly she said, "Yes, I think I would." That night after the show, the two of us sat in the theatre alone and the projectionist screened *Autumn Fire*. When it was over she wept, and two weeks later we were married. That's why I made the film. Having accomplished its purpose, it held no more interest for me. When friends would ask what I was doing I'd say, "Oh, writing a bit, and the theatre keeps me busy, and . . . oh, yes . . . I made a little film." "You made a little film!" they'd exclaim. "Let's see it!" So I'd show it to them. When they said how good it was and why didn't I show it, I said I didn't make it to show to anyone but one person and she saw it already. "Don't be ridiculous," they said, "nobody makes a film just for one person to see!" To which I replied, "And besides, it's very sentimental and romantic and —" "But *that's* what people like!" they'd say, "Show it and you'll see!" So I succumbed and

Autumn Fire (1930)

Autumn Fire (1980)

showed it and was pleasantly surprised to see that audiences did indeed like it. In due course I sent it to New York where it played in various little art cinemas there, finally to London and Paris, where it also showed in small theatres like the Little, showing avant-garde and experimental films. *Close-Up* magazine in Switzerland was so attracted by the stills of it I sent them that they ran two pages of them. (In 1970 when Henri Langlois put on a "60 Years of World Cinema" restrospective at the Musée d'Art Moderne in Paris, he asked for a print of *Autumn Fire* to be one of the films to represent the first American *avant-garde*. Since then it has become part of the archives of the National Film Archives of London, the Cinémathèque Française in Paris, the American Film Institute in Washington, and cinémathèques in Brussels, Vienna, Caracas, Rome, etc. (Here it is also in the archives of the Museum of Modern Art and the George Eastman House.)*

The year the Little Theatre opened, in the Winter of 1929, was the year that already witnessed the beginnings of the sound film, and although we began with the showing of silent films it wasn't long before we announced we were installing equipment to show sound films — the first booking being King Vidor's *Hallelujah*. But I couldn't wait to see it and I remember that one day (I already had the print from New York), when the screen and the horns were already up but the workmen were still hammering away at the boards holding the new screen, I told the projectionist to put the picture on while the men were still working on the screen, and so that's how I saw my first sound film — *Hallelujah* — as if I were seeing it during one of those modernist "constructivist" stage productions, such as Eisenstein used to mount for the Moscow Proletcult Theatre that they used to put on in the Soviet Union (Eisenstein once even staged a play set in a gas factory, in a real gas factory, to which the audience had to come). After that we showed some of the best sound films that were coming over from Europe (remember, we were primarily a European cinema house—in fact, shortly afterwards the name of the theatre was changed from the Little to the Europa.) Among the films we showed was

*In 1979 the Cinémathèque Suisse held an "hommage" to the Independent and avant-garde cinema of the silent era first celebrated at the Congress of La Sarraz in 1929, at which Eisenstein was the guest of honor; in it they showed *Autumn Fire* to represent, among others, the American avant-garde of '29.

Erna — after *Autumn Fire* (1931) (Photo by the author)

The Theft of the Mona Lisa (from Germany) with Willy Forst as an Italian glazier who, to impress a girl he's wooing, steals a small painting that he feels resembles her from the Louvre, none other than the "Mona Lisa," but when he discovers that she has gone off with her rich lover he brings it back, broken-hearted. It had a hit song, "Warum laechelst du, Mona Lisa?" (Why do you smile, Mona Lisa?)

A friend of mine, an art scholar from Italy, couldn't understand why everyone made such a fuss about the "mystery" of the Mona Lisa's smile in the famous Da Vinci painting. He said in Italy there was no mystery about it at all. Everyone knew, he said, that Da Vinci was a homosexual and that he had one of his boy friends pose for the portrait. The so-called "mysterious" smile on her face is just the smirk on the face of the young man sitting for the portrait which he knew was going to be that of a woman. An "in-joke" between Da Vinci and his boy friend, concluded my Italian friend, deadpan, thus became the most famous painting in the world.

I thought of him and his bizarre theory years later when Orson Welles told Michael MacLiammoir (who played Iago in Welles' film of *Othello*) in reply to MacLiammoir's thinking it was bizarre of Welles to cast the Negress Eartha Kitt as Helen in his projected production of *Dr. Faustus*, "Why?" Welles said, "Everyone knows Helen of Troy was colored."

We showed Hitchcock's *Juno and the Paycock*, from the searing O'Casey play on the Irish rebellion of 1916. "You're not goin' to do in an old comrade," pleads Johnny to the Irregulars who've come for him, "Look at me arm . . . I lost it for Ireland!" To which one of them replies, referring to a pal of Johnny's whom he unwittingly betrayed, "Commander Tancred lost his life for Ireland." "Haven't I done enough for Ireland?" cries out Johnny, waving the stump of his amputated arm. "No man," answers the other Irregular, "can do enough for Ireland." When Johnny's mother is informed of the execution of her son by the Sinn Feiners, "Mother of God, Mother of God!" she wails, "have pity on us all!" "Blessed Virgin!" she intones as she goes down the steps into the street, "where were you when me darlin' son was riddled with bullets?" (Sarah Allgood of the Abbey Theatre had the same role she did so eloquently on the stage.) "Take away our hearts of stone and give us hearts of flesh! Take away this murdherin' hate an' give us Thine own eternal love!" In all retrospectives of Hitchcock since, I have never once found this one by him included, for some mysterious reason that I never fathomed.

We showed John Ford's first sound film, *Men Without Women*, about sailors in a submarine that gets stuck and they have to "torpedo" the men out to save them — all but the last one — he is sacrificed for the sake of the others. It had a song, too, about a girl, whose heart was in the navy. "And all around her hips," one line went, "was a line of battle-ships . . ." She was, of course, tattooed. And as she undulated her hips, the warships seemed to be plowing through heavy seas. You really have to hear it all:

Oh I paid a shilling to see
The tattooed French lady,
Tattooed from head to knee,
She was a sight to see.
And all around her hips
Was a line of battleships,
And right above one kidney
Was a bird's eye view of Sidney;
But the one I like best
Was the view across her chest —
My home among the hills of old New Hampshire!

We showed Pabst's *The White Hell of Pitz Palu*, with Leni Riefenstahl and Gustav Diesl, filmed entirely in the wintry Alps, with a last minute air rescue by the famous German war ace, Ernst Udet, who was to become the real-life "Devil's General" that Carl Zuckmayer was later to dramatize. We showed *Zwei Herzen im dreiviertel Takt* (Two Hearts in Three-Quarter Time), the hit German musical — we showed many German musicals. What a time it was for them in the period of their florescence — 1930-32! *(Zwei Herzen* u.s.w. became the first of over 400 German, French, and Italian films I was to subtitle in English over the years that followed.) Snatches from some of them went . . .

From *Ein Maedel*
von der Reeperbahn   *Mach rot das Licht, wir wollen Tango*
tanzen, Ich und Du . . .
(Make the light red, we'll dance a
tango for them, I and you . . .)

From *Sein*
Liebeslied

Du bist meine Greta Garbo,
Bist die schoenste Frau der Welt,
Du schaust aus wie die Garbo,
Doch du hast nicht so viel Geld . . .
(You're my own, my Greta Garbo,
In all the world the prettiest
little honey,
You look just like Greta Garbo,
Only you haven't all her money . . .)

From *Die Lustigen*
Weiber von Wien

Ich liebe nur eine,
Die eine bist Du,
Sonst brauch ich keine,
  keine wozu —
Ich brauch nicht Kaiserin,
  Herzogin, Koenigin,
Ich brauch nur eine,
Die eine bist Du . . .
(I love but just one,
And that one is you;
I need no other, no other
  will do —
I don't need princesses,
  countesses, duchesses,
I need but just one and
That one is you!)

— and perhaps the most popular of them all —

From
Zwei Herzen
im ¾ Takt

Zwei Herzen im Dreivierteltakt,
Die hat der Mai zusammen gebracht;
Zwei Herzen im Dreivierteltakt
In einer grossen Nacht!
Ein Viertel Fruhling und ein Viertel
  Wein,
Ein Viertel Liebe, verliebt muss man
  sein . . .!
Zwei Herzen im Dreivierteltakt,
 Wer braucht mehr um gluecklich zu
  sein!

(freely)   (Two hearts in three-quarter time,
                        Who met one night in May;
                        Two hearts in three-quarter time
                        In a night supremely gay!
                        One quarter Springtime and one
                            quarter wine,
                        One quarter love for love makes it
                            divine . . .!
                        Two hearts then will everyone bless,
                        Who needs more for our happiness!)

There were dozens more — all in those blithe years 1930-32 — before Hitler screwed up Germany.

We showed Edouard Tissé's (Eisenstein's great cameraman) *Women's Weal, Women's Woe*, a film on childbirth, made by him with the cooperation of the Women's Hospital in Zurich for the Swiss producer of so many good films, Lazare Wechsler. It was made by Tissé to earn some money for him, Alexandrov and Eisenstein on their way from Moscow to Paris. We showed Pabst's *Westfront 1918*, a searing film about the First World War from Germany and very anti-war, again with Gustav Diesl. We showed *The Tempest** with Emil Jannings and Anna Sten (my, but she was good-looking in those days!). We also showed her and Fritz Kortner in a Russo-German adaptation of *The Brothers Karamazov* by Fedor Ozep, with a stunning music score by Karol Rathaus, a model of its kind. *"Romeo von Funfundsechszig Jahren!"* says Ivan contemptuously about his father's passion for Gruschenka. ("Romeo at 65 years of age!") Dmitri needs money from his father for Gruschenka. Ivan doubts he will get it. *"Gibt der Vater das Geld?"* he asks Smerdyakov. ("Will father give it to him?") *"Der Vater braucht selbst das Geld,"* whines Smerdyakov. ("Father needs the money himself.") They all need it for the same purpose — for Gruschenka, the father's mistress. This was the role Marilyn Monroe wanted so much to play. And when Dmitri confronts Ivan after his first visit to Gruschenka (they're playing at billiards), Dmitri says, *"Ich bin zu Gruschenaka gekommen und jetzt is alles vorbei—Katja, der Dienst—und die Ehre!"* He bends down to make a shot, gets up and repeats — *"Ja, wenn du willst — auch die Ehre!"* ("I went to Grushenka and now

---

*Reversing the usual process of title changes in America, the original German title for *The Tempest* was *Sturm der Leidenschaft* (Storm of Passion).

everythings's lost — Katia" — his betrothed — "the Service — and my honor! Yes, if you want it all — my honor, too!") There was a deliciously ironic moment when Dmitri berates Gruschenka for carrying on like a young whore at her age — "A girl of 18!" — to which Gruschenka objects. *"Seventeen!"* she cries out, not wishing to be thought older than she is.

We showed *Maedchen in Uniform, Lot in Sodom, Le Million* of René Clair, *Das Lied vom Leben* (The Song of Life) by Granowsky of the Moscow Academic Theatre, an ode to youth from a script by Victor Trivas who collaborated also on such sterling works as Ozep's *Karamazov* film, Pabst's *The Love of Jeanne Ney*, and directed one of the most striking anti-war films, *Niemandsland* (No Man's Land). In *Das Lied vom Leben*, a girl runs away from marriage to a rich old man and runs to her young man. They have a child and an amazing sequence follows devoted to the child — and what a child means. As it cries, we see the screen literally swarming with people, thousands and thousands of them, while off screen a voice intones: *"Hoeren sie, wie es schrie?"* ("Do you hear how it cries?") And then to the child, *"Du bist auf dieser Erde nicht allein!"* ("You are not alone on this earth!") Then the young mother, cradling the child in her arms, insists that *"Baby bleibt immer Baby!"* ("Baby will always remain Baby!") To which the father says, as we see a low sailors' dive somewhere — Port Saïd, Marseilles or Hong Kong — *"Baby wird ein grosser Mann sein, mit ein grossen Bart . . ."* ("Baby will become a big man with a big beard . . .") And he'll meet women, women galore — *"Weisse, und Schwarze und Gelbe . . ."* ("White, Black and Yellow . . .") The songs and recitatives were by Hans Eisler.

We showed Elizabeth Bergner in her first sound film *Ariane*, also about a young girl's first love (everything seemed dedicated to youth in those days tho' not the way they do it today but lyrically). In June of 1937, the following year, I received a copy of Claude Anet's novel, *Ariane: Jeune Fille Russe*, inscribed to me by my brother: *"A Herman, parce qu'il connait Ariane aussi bien que Claude Anet — et parce qu'il cherche encore la vrai Ariane."* — Max, 6/12/37. That will give you an idea of how I was carrying on about Erna . . . We showed *The Constant Nymph*, from the novel by Margaret Kennedy, musicals like *Die Lustigen Weiber von Wien* (The Merry Wives of Vienna, *Drei von der Tankstelle* (Three from the Gas Station), *Die Dreigroschenoper*, with Lotte Lenya, the first Soviet

Inaugurating the 1932-33 Season — The Little Theatre (now the Europa) as the author raises a sidewalk easel to shield the carbon-arc light from a sudden shower. The diaphanous figure behind the left door is Erna. (Collection of the author)

sound film about the *besprezhornie*, the wild boys left in the backwash of the war, *The Road to Life*, the French *Crime and Punishment* (the best one ever), with Harry Baur as Porfiry and Pierre Blanchar as Raskolnikov. When Porfiry plays his cat and mouse game with Raskolnikov, he finally gets Raskolnikov so exasperated that Raskolnikov says, "Well then, who do *you* think did it?" Porfiry smiles and points furtively at Raskolnikov and with a smile quietly says, "You." We also showed Pabst's *Kameradschaft* (Comradeship) about the Courriers mine tragedy when the German miners went to the rescue of the French miners working a section of the mine over the French border and saved them after a tunnel collapsed. There was a magnificent scene where an entombed French miner is tapping, tapping to bring attention to his plight, when a German fellow miner reaches him by boring through solid rock with a drill hammer and as the German miner rushes in to save the French miner we see on the screen not the two miners but two soldiers, French and German, on the Western Front, locked in each others' arms, the drill-hammer having become a machine-gun as the two struggle — an hallucination, of course, of the French miner . . . In the end, the officials put up the barriers between the German and French sections of the mine, the "borderline," as before.

It was a six-day-a-week theatre because Sundays we were closed, on account of "the blue laws." "Blue" meant something else then — sadness. So Sundays we (Erna and I) went out into the country or to Washington — via car, we had a friend with a car.

We were on our way to Washington once, being driven by our friend, to have dinner at Harvey's, noted for its sea-food, though why anyone should leave Baltimore where the best sea-food on the Eastern Coast was available, is beyond me, now that I look back at it. There must have been a reason — I guess it was the pleasant ride. We used to make the trip quite often on Sundays when "the blue laws' kept theatres closed — mustn't have any wicked goings-on on the Sabbath, you know. Anyway, whatever the reason, this time it wasn't chance but Fate, mis-named . . . as it always is . . . and as Stroheim had already pointed out in *The Wedding March* . . .

We passed a field on which we saw an airplane next to a sign saying, "Take a Flight — $5.00," and Erna cried out, "Stop the car! I wanna fly!" The car screeched to a stop. "I've never been

A Curtiss "Jenny", vintage of 1912, combat plane of the First World War, in which the author took his first (and last) flight. (1931) (New York Public Library — Picture Collection)

up in a plane," she said, delightedly, "come on!" And she began pulling me out of the car. "No, you don't wanna fly," I said, "Yes, I do!" she said. "I never been up!" and she pulled me across the field while our friend, smiling at the way we were carrying on, waited by the roadside. I guess he had no interest in flying, either, like me. "Barnstormers," they were called, ex-pilots of World War I, who couldn't get a job, used to rent old bi-planes, usually former military craft, and take passengers up for a five or ten minute spin for five to ten dollars, or they'd give exhibitions at fairs of climbing, diving, doing barrelrolls and the rest. It was a living and here I was about to be tested for that myself. And now, there she was, a Curtiss Jenny, vintage of even before the First World War, 1912, the pilot said.

There were places for two in the open cockpits — pilot and observer — but the front observer's cockpit was to contain us both, me and her on my lap. I found out later you weren't supposed to do this* but, as far as I was concerned, even without knowing that then, things were hazardous enough for me. As I was being strapped in and fitted with goggles and a leather flier's helmet I began thinking of my happy life until that moment and what was I doing here being put at the mercy of this dubious looking contraption that was to "have it out" with the theory of aerodynamics (a theory I could not then and still cannot understand)? I even thought I was beginning to see my past life starting to unreel before me. And it was only when Erna said, as she was about to be settled on my lap, "Get that out of my way," that I realized I'd taken my camera along, a small Kodak "Brownie" box camera of the time, "Ah," said the pilot. "You've got a camera? Good! We'll take pictures when we get over the capitol." And he took the camera. I'd never been up before either and had not the slightest curiosity as to what flying was like. And here I was, willy-nilly, going to get it in full measure. And just married, too! What a pity . . .!

An angry sputter of engine and sudden roar of whirling pro-

*In that model of patrician prose put to the service of an account of a trans-Sahara expedition, Lord Norwich in *Sahara* (New York, 1968) notes the seating of Captain Laperrine, commander for France of the *Territoires du Sud* in the North Africa of 1920, in the front open cockpit on the observer's knee in a little two-seater Breguet bi-plane. I note this only to show that physically it can be done, although it is foolhardy to do it. (Laperrine was mortally hurt when a sudden up-draft of hot air off the sand overturned the plane and it crashed, pinning Laperrine under the fuselage, though the observer and pilot both escaped unhurt.)

peller, a rush of high wind in the face, and we were off, the earth sinking below us, lower and lower. "Wheee!" she exclaimed, "Isn't it marvelous!" Then I turned and saw the pilot, in the cockpit behind us, holding the camera. "Never mind the camera!" I shouted over the propeller's roar but I knew he couldn't hear me. Erna pointed to the inter-com and I picked it up and repeated, *"Never-mind-the-camera!* Put your hands back on the stick!" The primitive planes of the time were guided, raised and lowered, by a control stick coming up from the floor of the cockpit — and there he was, both hands holding the camera, looking around for good shots. Desperately I shouted over the inter-com, "There's no film in the camera, anyway!"

"What d'ya mean there's no film in the camera?" came back his voice. "Of course there is! I can see the number one on the roll!" Now he was exasperated. "And stop bothering me, you're making me nervous!" he said. "Did you hear that?" said Erna. "He said you should cut it out, you're making him nervous!"

Mercy me! *I* didn't want to make the pilot nervous, that's the last thing on earth I would do at a time like this! "What's the matter?" smiled Erna. "You look green around the gills." I attempted a faint smile but my heart wasn't in it. I'd left my heart down on earth, hugging the ground, kissing the greensward. "If we ever get out of this trap in one piece," I shouted at her (god-damn that propeller and the barrage it was making!) "I'll never try it again! Never! He hasn't even got his hand on the stick, he's taking pictures!" "Oh look," she said, "there's the Washington Monument!" "Where?" I said, looking around. "I don't see a thing." "Down there, stupid!" she said, pointing towards the earth and I looked down. A tiny toothpick of a white shaft thrust itself upward from what seemed like miles below. I was beyond words. A silly thought kept whirling about me — "Whom the gods love die young" — it went. Followed by — "A short life and a merry one" — and then we dropped, we plummeted straight down until the plane leveled off again and now we were over the dome of the capitol building, quite low, too . . .

I remember nothing else till we got back to our take-off field. The pilot cut his engine. When the sputter of the propeller stopped it was all quiet again — blessed quiet. The pilot got out and came up to us, helping Erna, then me, down. The rapture with which my feet felt the ground again can't be described. Erna was thanking the pilot for a "lovely ride" and our friend by the car came over to greet us. "Why did we drop?" I managed to ask the pilot when I could catch my breath. "Oh that," he said. "Air pocket — it's nothing — happens all the time — a vacuum in the air . . ." "Oh," I said, as if that explained everything.*

"Wasn't that great?" said Erna to me, as we walked towards the car. I managed a smile and nodded. "My first and last flight," I said. "Oh, come on!" she insisted, "You'll get used to it, if you give yourself a chance. You know what you should do? Next Sunday we'll drive out here and go up again —" At which I started to laugh and so did she and our friend too. The pilot, if he was looking our way, must have seen three jolly people getting in the car, laughing their heads off, and driving away.**

Not only don't I fly, I don't drive a car either. I can only do things (or at least attempt them) that allow a wide margin for error — like writing books. Which reminds me of an incident apropos that took place years later, recently in fact. One dusk found me wending my way homeward when I passed a girl walking over to a car that had drawn up at the curb, apparently to answer the invitation of the young man at the wheel to join him, I gathered. Being curious if she would, I kept looking back, the while proceeding on my way while watching their

---

*This was different from a down-draft, I learned later, which can do the same thing.

**It was, indeed, my first and last flight. I haven't flown since. And by the way, the pictures the pilot took came out fine. But when I read that George S. Kaufman, who also didn't fly, started a club for non-fliers called *The Newton Was Right Club*, I began to keep a record of all those I heard did not fly and were charter members of that club. To date that list includes (besides me): Al Hirschfeld, Salvador Dali, Bert Lahr, Rita Hayworth, Vladimir Horowitz, Leopold Stokowski, Gloria Swanson, Marcel Pagnol, Lucius Beebe, Ogden Nash, J. Edgar Hoover, Oscar Levant, Somerset Maugham, Evel Knievel, Ernest Boyd, Ermano Olmi, E.B. White, Stanley Kubrick, Isaac Asimov, Alain Robbe-Grillet, S.M. Behrman, James Agate, Duke Ellington, S.J. Perleman, Roland Topor, Mae West, Monica Vitti, Anna Magnani, Peter Finch, Ingmar Bergman, Irving Wallace, Jean Renoir, Alberto Ginastero, Dmitri Shostakovich, James Cagney, Aldo Ciccolini, Joanne Woodward, Joan Baez, Tony Curtis, Mike Douglas, Joan Crawford, Maureen Stapleton, Glen Gould, Andre Previn, Ray Bradbury, Ian Fleming, Shelly Berman, Jackie Gleason, Henny Youngman, Ronald Reagan (in the old days), Erica Jong, Bella Abzug, Leo Ornstein, J. Paul Getty, Mamie Eisenhower, Hermione Gingold, Huntington Hartford, John Galsworthy, King Vidor. There are some listed here who have since died, but not from flying.

conversation. As she got in the car I stumbled over the guard-rail around a tree and toppled over, sprawling full length on the sidewalk. A passerby helped me up, and outside of a bumped knee and a bruised jaw I was alright. The moral was obvious: look where you're going, but that didn't occur to me as I watched the car with the girl inside drive off. All I could think of was: why didn't I ever learn to drive a car?

Of days spread like peacock tails,
Of days worn savagely like parrot feathers . . .

(Kay Boyle)

"Le Sacre du Printemps — or Charles Street on Saturday Night" . . . I called it when I sent it off to the Seven Arts Feature Syndicate . . . Charles Street, the Madison Avenue of Baltimore, Madison Avenue from the Fifties to the Eighties . . .

When he and she stand on the corner
holding hands and gazing abstractedly at
each other, neither of them speaking —
When she stands stubbornly on the side-
walk after he has gotten into the car —
When they begin to drift unsteadily
down the steps at Lee Turner's —
When the parked automobiles disclose
in their shadows living tableaux of
Rodin's "Le Printemps Eternel" —
When rosebuds are gathered in the
dark recesses of the Washington Monument —
Or by the fountain, or before the
monument in Washington Square —
When she yells an all-inclusive
greeting to a new party of arrivals as
she leaves the Belvedere Bar —
And when the newcomers, none of whom
know her, answer her greeting —
When a passing roadster lets out a
war hoop as it passes MacGillivry's —
Or when she cries out, "Let's have one
more," coming out of the Stafford
Bar —
Or furtively follows him into the hall-
way in the 900 block —
Or lets out a burp as she brings up her
hand, holding a lighted cigarette to her

mouth in embarrassment, as she staggers
up the steps of the Siegfried-Stube —
    When they begin to sing off-key at
Jack and Gill's —
    And heads are invariably raised to
see if Manly's is still there —
    When he gets lit on two beers and
feels like Casanova and she feels like
Constance Bennett —
    And it's warm outside, and the next
day is Sunday anyway, and he says "Well
are you going to stand there all night?"
and she feels like crying, and now her whole
week-end is ruined —
    When Bul-Bul* and the doves of Mount
Vernon Place have gone to sleep and the
last night plane from Logan Field zooms
across the sky and hushed feminine mur-
murs come through the dark opened windows
of the bachelor apartments —
    And a lone couple walk hand in hand
down the street —
    As the first faint streaks of dawn
creep over the roof-tops —
    And it begins to
drizzle — and
they hail a
cab —
    And decide, finally, to call it a
night —
    Spring has come to Charles Street!

The first and last couples in this "dizzyramb" being, of course, Erna and me.

Oh yes, and we were closed in the summer, too — did I forget to say that? For the simple reason that we had no cooling system (we weren't up to the words "air-conditioning" yet — that was a classy Forties phrase) so — what did we do in the summer? I went up to New York and spent the summer titling foreign films for non-linguistic American movie audiences — *Two Hearts in Waltz Time, The Merry Wives of Vienna* . . . If

*Siegfried Weisberger's spaniel.

Baltimore — Winter of 1935. Winter also came to Charles Street. Charles Street, Corner of Mulberry. The circular marquee of Hopper Mcgaw's is visible on the right. (Photo: Aubrey Bodine) (New York Public Library — Picture Collection)

everybody thinks *My Fair Lady* was a scrumptious musical show — it was, it was! — but you still should have seen *The Merry Wives of Vienna*, with a rapturous music score by Robert Stolz and with Willy Forst, Liane Haid, Paul Hoerbiger and Oskar Sima, my goodness what a knockout of a musical! And I don't think it's been revived once since. *Maedchen in Uniform, The Three-Penny Opera, The Private Secretary*, with the delicious Renate Mueller, before Goebbels hounded her to suicide . . . u.s.w. from Germany. *Mayerling, Un Carnet de Bal, A Nous la Liberté, Harvest*, the *Marius-Fanny-César* trilogy of Marcel Pagnol, *Sous les Toits de Paris, Le Rosier de Madame Huson**, with the irrepressible Fernandel after a Maupassant bawdy joke and with director Bernard Deschamps doing a "French Lubitsch turn," with my definition, via a subtitle, of a pure or virgin girl (which was what the story's about) as being "a girl where the hand of man had never never set foot," Dreyer's *Vampyr*, if you can imagine a tale of vampires and an ambiance of suppressed dread done with the airiest charm, interiors as if by Vuillard and exteriors as if by Monet and Pissarro, etc. . . . from France. (By the time I titled my last foreign film, *The Little Theatre of Jean Renoir*, in 1971, I had performed this office upon well over 400 films from abroad, including Sicilian, Japanese, Swedish, Hindustani, Spanish, Brazilian, Greek, Finnish, Yugoslavian, Czech, Hungarian —everything but Swahili. The secret of it all lay in the translator's first rule as formulated by H.G. Wells, to wit, that "It's more important to have a wider knowledge of the language you are going into than the language you are coming from." Of course, you have to know where you're coming from, too, but one is more important than the other. There's lots more involved in all this, the other rules of which I'll spare you.

So nights I prowled around Times Square, when that place was more or less new to me (in 1930 I was 22), and once I even sent back a "New York Letter" to the Seven Arts people . . . my *sturm und drang* period, as you can see, but it was New York as I saw it in 1931, nevertheless . . .

NEW YORK LETTER

Times Square — that vortex of the city's metropolitan life — throbs nightly like the beating of an overstrained heart. It radiates a superabundant energy which seems

---

*An especial favorite of Fritz Lang.

directed toward setting some huge metaphorical ferris wheel in motion. It is like a long lane of booths at a circus fair — with the perennial "barkers" bellowing forth their wares:

"The hottest show in town — new performance starts in five minutes — get your seats now!"

" — step up this way and get a nice cool Honeymoon drink —"

"Going right in now for a complete new show . . ."

". . . right inside, the best dance floor in town, only 25 cents . . ."

"Goin' right out to Coney Island, 75ᶜ a round trip . . . goin' right out."

". . . morning paper, nurse slashes doctor's throat with razor . . . get your morning paper . . ."

" — so I sez to him, sez I . . ."

"Buy a pencil . . . buy a pencil" — and the dull thud of the blind man's stick on the sidewalk as the wild-eyed crowd of pleasure-seekers, racketeers, ogling visitors and yokels, shop girls, tarts and aimless strollers, make way for him.

In the hotels, elevators discharge their cargo of guests into their lobbies — like so many dinosaur eggs which hatch their motley brood at regular intervals . . .

Outside, the street traffic is unceasing as it is enormous. All the taxicabs of the world seem to have collected here for a perennial sweepstakes. The feeling in safely having crossed a street is not in having succeeded because of the perspicacity of the taxi-driver, but in having outwitted him by the most cunning dexterity.

Still the swarm of seething humanity — like bees around a honeycomb, like moths around the ol' flame . . .

. . . Over and above all a hazy mist like illuminated gold dust hangs in the air. Above even that is the deep blue sky and the stars. From the river the blast of a departing liner is heard along the docksides . . .

Down at the Battery, the sea-gulls are flying low over the softly lapping waves in the moonlight. Far away is the madness, the cruelty and urgency of New York in a blaze of incandescent light which is Times Square.

Only here, at night alone, is there a feeling of peace and quiet, an almost tremulous repose. Here, besides the shadowy, inchoate and amorphous forms of slumbering skyscrapers which rise up from the sea like the prows of huge ships . . .

Passing out through the Narrows, a departing liner can be seen, edging her way out of the bay into the expanse of the Atlantic — her decks ablaze, her sides studded with tiny points of light like flashing diamonds.

And turning back, there are New York's four huge suspension bridges, stretching out their steel arms as if in an embrace, like some senseless mother watching over her brood at night as they sleep . . .

Meanwhile, Erna remained in Baltimore. We lived then on that handsome square, at 12 West Mount Vernon Place, while the family lived at 12 East Mount Vernon Place, that quadrangle of greensward from which the Washington Monument jutted straight up and around which a festive flower show took place every year . . . Mount Vernon Place, Baltimore's equivalent to London's Trafalgar Square, around which were gathered the Peabody Conservatory of Music and the fabulous Walters Art Gallery . . . the place that Mencken once called, in one of his periodic states of euphoria, one of the most beautiful squares in the world . . .

Erna chided me for leaving her alone so much. She was right, of course. But the world was full of so many interesting people and things. Still, I said I was sorry and that from now on I would make it up to her. Before I had a chance, chance itself intervened to take a hand in shaping what was to follow. Through chance I had won her and now through that same quirk of fate I was going to lose her.

Among the doctors I used to meet in that city of doctors, that city of Osler, Halsted, Kelly, Welch and Garrison — by virtue of the great Johns Hopkins Hospital there — was Dr. Shoye Yamauchi, resident surgeon at Mount Sinai Hospital nearby. Dr Yamauchi, who was to become instrumental in making the next change in the course of my life, just as Erna had inadvertently made the first change. This was just as inadvertent. Funny how fate arranges things to make it all seem to happen by the merest chance. It began with our inviting him to our place. He was a handsome young Hawaiian-Japanese who, after interning at Mt. Sinai, became resident surgeon there and was Erna's doctor when she entered the hospital for the correction of some minor ailment. When we were married,

Mount Vernon Place — Baltimore (1932) (Photo by Aubrey Bodine)
© W.W. Norton (New York Public Library — Picture Collection)

he sent us a book as a wedding gift, tales of the South Seas, inscribed "May time keep you both always to delight in simple tales." On his visits, he would bring Japanese records (I remember one, "The Old Castle," sung by Yoshi Fujiwara, a sad song about an old ruined castle in the moonlight where happy people once lived, now abandoned and inhabited only by ghosts.) He brought picture books about Japan and Hawaii. He'd arrive sometimes as I was leaving for the theatre, after dinner, in the early evening. Or I'd meet him leaving, as I was returning from the theatre. Where, or how, I got the notion that all this traffic to and fro on his part "quite obviously" meant that there was something between them, I don't know. I didn't know it then and I still don't know it. I must have seen too many movies, I'm sure I saw too many movies, as a result of which I was addled with romantic notions. Whatever it was, I felt hurt — or, let us say, I thought I felt hurt. What's the difference? When I offered to give her her freedom to do as she liked, she seemed surprised. How can one know these things when one is as addle-pated as I must have been from seeing so many movies, even good movies? Characters were always making noble sacrifices in the movies, and all that . . . At any rate, she said she wouldn't stand in my way, that I should feel free to do as I like. We were both offering each other freedom to act as we pleased. How's that for nobility? Talk about the movies! Life isn't like the movies, but we didn't know that.* We were both trying to be correct, if you please. According to those goddamned movies. And so, while I was under that spell, acting in all righteousness without a shred of real, not fancied, evidence, I called in a lawyer friend (the brother of that fellow who used to belt out, oh Christ! *Last night, ah, yesternight, betwixt her lips and mine* . . .) and asked him to institute divorce proceedings, whereupon he reminded me that you couldn't get a divorce in Maryland save on one ground — adultery — at which point irony spat in my eye. This could be "arranged," of course through collusion, wherein one party takes the rap and the other accuses the other. Silly, but that's the way it was. So it was drawn up that she accused me and, since I did not dispute the accusation, she was awarded a divorce — as simple as it was silly.

*"If there's something I hate, it's the movies," says Holden Caufield in *Catcher in the Rye*. "Don't even mention them to me. They can ruin you!"

Having acted so damned "honorably," I felt in the days that followed like a bloody martyr. The "frost of knighthood" was in my manner. But who needed it? In short, I was feeling terrible. I had written to that fourth girl, whom Erna had replaced, but whose address I had kept (make something out of that, you Freudians) and now, belatedly (my, how screwy things could get in those blithe days), she had her job replacing Erna as cashier.

And as I was sitting in my office in the theatre one day, ruminating on the vagaries of life, the door suddenly opened, and who should breeze in? Erna, good old Erna! It was just like that morning a century before (that's what it seemed like, so much had happened since then) when she first came barging up the stairs to ask if the job as usherette was still open. I got up and rushed over to her and embraced here. "Hello, darling," I said. I'd have given my soul to have her back again at that moment! But she broke away. I was desperate. "Remember . . .?" I began, but she put her gloved finger to my lips to hush me up. There were to be no reminiscences. Then she said it, in Russian, a language she rarely used, whispering it in my ear — *"Proschaite."* She had come to say goodbye . . .

Jean-Paul Sartre tells an anecdote about himself, that he was about to descend from a train once when he noticed a girl, an extremely pretty girl, running towards him. He knew she was running towards *him* because he was the only one descending from that *wagon-lit*. His heart, he said, leaped in anticipation — he had made a conquest! When she came up to him, she handed him a book and asked him, breathlessly, if he'd please autograph her copy of his latest book, upon which his heart sank and the rest of his day was ruined.

That's how I felt at that moment. She had not come to say, "I can't! I can't!" (Oh, couldn't she, though? She not only could but she did. She saw the "blocks" falling into place, the "steppingstone blocks" on which she could elevate herself from movie cashier to the wife of a doctor who would take her to Honolulu. All girls know just what they are doing and why. They're shrewd but then they have to be. They can't leave it to the men.) She had come just to say, *"Proschaite . . ."* — goodbye. Not only did she seldom speak Russian but I'd never even heard her speak her native tongue, Latvian, and, curiously, at that moment I wondered what it sounded like. What did it matter now *what* it sounded like? I tried again. "Remember that abacus you brought in that day . . .?" I began. "I was kidding," she smiled. "Sure," I said. "But you had me worried for a while . . ." "Did I?" she smiled. "You certainly did," I said. We'd been through so much together. "Thanks for everything," she murmured, and before I could say another word she rushed out of the office. I stood there for what must have been a long time, dazed, feeling I would probably never see her again, feeling — not even a goodbye kiss — nor a last embrace . . . even Josefina had kissed me goodbye that last night in Havana. *Never??* Never is a long time . . . it's as long a time as there is. They say that to part is to die a little. A bit of me has died that way many times. Can't be very much left . . .

I remembered that one night I had taken her to a midnight sailing to see a friend off on the "Ile de France" at the French Line pier in New York. It was the director, Bob Florey and his pretty wife, Virginia. They were going to France. The pier was jammed with well-wishers seeing friends and relatives off. Thousands of paper streamers seemed to be holding the ship fast to the shore — streamers that each had thrown, the departing passengers to their loved ones they were leaving behind and those on the pier to those they had come to see off, standing by the ship's rails and calling out last farewells. Then over their cries the long low mournful blast of the ship's fog-horn sounded and the great liner began to move away, breaking the paper streamers that were meant to keep her there, to never let her part, breaking every last one of them as she inched out of her pier while all around us were eyes full of tears . . .

"You see," I said to her, "that's how it is to part." Her only answer was to hug my arm a little tighter.

That's how it was to part.

Years later, in The Christian Science Monitor, I found an echo of that night in a poem by Margaret Tsuda . . .

> It was raining and
>   we were late into the boat.
> Paper streamers
>   were already being hurled
>   from deck to dock.
> I saw a young man
>   catch one and
>   hold on even as
>   our boat veered seaward.

Unheeding of rains and
  inky waters turbulent below
  he ran out to the very
  edge of the pier
  until
  his fragile paper
  bridge-line snapped.
Our life experience is
  filled with such partings,
  not usually acted out
  with such
  visible symbols . . .
One departs —
  one remains
Each has one-half of a
  brightly colored
  streamer of memories
  for
  cherishing.

Years later, when I revisited Baltimore with my daughter, Gretchen, for the first time since I left in 1936 (I shouldn't have gone; Thomas Wolfe was right, you can't go back — everything degenerates), I told her I'd show her the place where I had lived. We took a cab to Mount Vernon Place and got out at the monument. I started walking, rather briskly as I remember, and finally stopped and looked up. I shuddered when I realized I was in front of 12 West Mount Vernon Place, where I lived briefly with Erna, not 12 East, where I lived with my family for long (three years) after I broke with Erna, where I had *meant* to take Gretchen. How's that for a little ghost story? I shouldn't have gone back. For me it was all ghosts there.*
I had stayed on for three more years, from 1933 to '36, haunted by the memory of her, turning over and over again in my mind the latest news I had had of her, that she and Dr. Yamauchi had gone to his home in Honolulu where they married. By 1936 I'd had enough of old haunts and old memories and returned to New York. But years later (my, how the time goes by!) when a friend of mine, John Turner, was going on a trip to

*As for the degeneracy, there are no words to describe what happened to the once lovely Little Theatre as I knew it.

Japan (he said he'd heard of a place there where they cultivated black roses, no less, and being an amateur tho' avid horticulturist he wanted to see them and bring some back), I asked him to phone Erna in Honolulu and give her greetings and good wishes from me. I looked up Dr. Yamauchi in the Honolulu phone book and there he was, and since all flights to Japan made a fuel stop in Hawaii, I felt my friend would be able to accomplish his mission.

He told me when he returned (without the black roses, alas) that, yes, he had called her to say he was bringing greetings from me and that I wished her well, thinking she might invite him to tea. He had a camera along to take a picture of her, which I had asked him to do and which I wanted very much to see because I'd been told that white women living in the Orient for any length of time invariably lost their good looks, if they were attractive to begin with — as in that cruel story, *Red*, by Somerset Maugham — but she hesitated when she heard the reason for the call. Hesitated, my foot, there was a long pause, my friend said, and then she said softly, "Ah, yes — but that was a long time ago . . ." And so he didn't get invited and couldn't take the picture . . .

> *Dans le vieux parc solitaire et glacé*
> *Deux spectres ont évoqué le passé . . .*
>
> (Verlaine)

> —*Do you remember our old ecstacies?*
> —*Why would you have me waken those memories?*
> —*When you hear my name does your heart always glow?*
>   *Do you always see my soul in dreams? — No.*
> —*Ah, the good days of joys unspeakable*
>   *when our lips mingled! — That is possible.*
> —*How blue the sky was then, and hope beat high!*
> —*But hope fled, vanquished, down the gloomy sky . . .*
> *Even so they walked through the wild oats, these dead,*
> *and only the night heard the words they said.*

After going through a period of "reaction" during which I vowed I was "through with women" (I played the Dietrich record, *Peter*, over and over again, her "repentant" song, as an antidote to the bitchy "triumphant" one, *Jonny*, and going through my head were Langston Hughes' lines from that distraught mother . . .

I'll nevah let mah chile love a man,
I said, I'll nevah let mah chile love
  a man,
'Cause love can hurt you
Mo' than anythin' else can!)

I returned to the 55th St. Playhouse in New York where it all started, only to find a pair of merry dark eyes on one of the usherettes (my, how that institution of "Usherettes" tossed me about!) and, thinking there was no harm in proposing that she sup with me, following the classic opening wedge, "What are you doing after the show?" (which doubtless has shaped many an unwitting man's future) — even though I was "through with women" (yea, in the proverbial pig's eye, I was*, at least not for one more round) — she accepted.

That did it. The rest became the real thing for which her predecessor had been only a practice run, so to speak, but that, as they say, is another story.

Tho' what a practice run!

---

*Which reminds me that at one point in a film she was doing with John Huston (I think it was *Night of the Iguana*), Ava Gardner let out with "In a pig's ass!", whereupon director Huston stopped the cameras, went over to her, and putting his arm around her said, "No, honey, not 'In a pig's ass,' 'In a pig's eye will do quite nicely."

Some thoughts to the click of the wheels on the Baltimore & Ohio train from Baltimore to New York, Summer of 1936 . . .

The thought while re-reading Oscar Wilde's fervid ode to Christ, *Salome*, that with Charles Laughton as Herod, Conrad Veidt as Jokanaan, and Constance Bennett or Miriam Hopkins as Salome, the result would be worth going miles to see.

The Walpurgis Nacht chapter of Mann's *The Magic Mountain*, particularly Hans Castorp's last plea to the lovely Clavdia Chauchat beginning *"Oh, l'amour, tu sais — Le corps, l'amour, la mort, ces trois ne font qu'un . . ."*

Clavdia Chauchat, Ariane Kutznetsova, Stasha von Luiwenhuk, Concha Perez and Paprika — five of the most exciting heroines in modern literature.

Hinda Wasau, Ina Ray Hutton, Marlene Dietrich, Elisabeth Bergner and Polly Walters — five of the most exciting heroines in the modern theatre. (Dietrich had played both Stasha von Luiwenhuk and Concha Perez, and could do Clavdia Chauchat with no effort at all; Bergner had done Ariane Kutznetsova; and it is but a toss-up between Hinda Wasau and Polly Walters for the role of Paprika.)

James Branch Cabell's *Thirst for Purple Things*. Disraeli's little known discourse on the same subject. Catulle Mendes' *Melicerte*.

An exquisite film, *Marie*, that we screened privately, directed by Paul Fejos, starring Annabella, which America will never see because through the stupid and impudent action of the New York censors it was banned on the grounds that "it makes a mockery of religion, the administration of justice and the conduct of respectable society, generally." In the opinion of at least this observer, so long as *Marie* is banned then so long will the censors themselves have condemned their own existence.

Its plot was the simplest:

A peasant girl in a village in Hungary is seduced by the local farm bailiff, becomes pregnant, and is driven by her shame from the village to the town. There she becomes a servant in a disreputable café and brothel. The authorities try to remove her child to an orphanage but she resists. In a church, in hysterics, she bewails to the Virgin Mary, "You were allowed to keep your child, why can't I keep mine?" In her misery she dies, but, having been a good girl, goes to Heaven, where she is happy again in her old job as a maid in a heavenly kitchen with gold utensils. One day she looks down on the Earth and sees her daughter, now grown to young and pretty womanhood, flirting at a garden gate with a young man who seems very taken with her and even tries to kiss her. The girl's mother in heaven gets panicky — she doesn't want her daughter tricked into her own fate. Desperately she looks around the kitchen and finds a pail which she fills with water and, just as her daughter is about to succumb to the young man's ardor, she pours the pail of water down on the couple below, where it suddenly starts to rain. At this, the daughter runs into the house and the young man runs off. The mother, triumphant, looks down, beaming.

The night Heifetz appeared with the Philharmonic under Toscanini playing the Beethoven Violin Concerto and the next two hours after that . . . that forty minute all-time record by motor car to Washington, New Year's Eve, 1930 . . . that misty return from Washington one Sunday by motor, in which heaven and earth merged to one . . . New Year's Eve 1931 in the 1100 block North Charles Street, sandwiched in between *Frankenstein* at Keith's and herring at the Riviera (to snap out of a hangover), but New Year's Eve in the 1100 block North Charles Street, none-the-less . . . that night when I left a bunch of the boys on Monument Street and came back, instinctively, for one more "goodnight" — one of the sanest moves I ever made . . . the long fascinating sessions from midnight to dawn scoring silent films . . . the Saturday night get-togethers in the 700 block North Howard Street . . . the parties thrown around screenings, that good old Hardman Peck and non-synch machine . . . blackjack and the insoluble problem of whether to draw on sixteen . . . bootleg rye and bathtub gin, week-ends, the Jefferson at Atlantic City, Room 2110, nocturnal prowlings on Fayette Street, the Oasis on East Baltimore St., usherettes — Polish, Russian, German, Danish . . . FIRE! . . . everybody is a hero . . . parades . . . shooting *Autumn Fire* . . . German musical films . . . *Pitz Palu, Sein Liebeslid, Die Lindenwirtin, Hungarian Rhapsody, A Royal Scandal, Two Hearts, Das Lied von Leben* . . . Kaleidoscope of events, whispered promises, appointments, rendezvous, performance starts at 2, Sundays off, dinners at the K. of C., Ortman's, Harvey's, Howard and Franklin, film shunting through the machines night and day, watched over by those two master minds, projectionists Bill and Charley, the days and nights growing into weeks and months to the clicking of the intermittent sprockets spinning the hours now crowded with reminiscence . . .

Six weeks I was to have stayed and now it was six years later. Memory, said Jean Paul, is "the one beautiful paradise from which we cannot be expelled." And if it were not for memory, who could say that we had lived?

OLD SONGS — OLD LOVES

ETTA & GRETCHEN (1936-1950)

The term "godfather" is used more loosely now than in its original meaning. Whatever it meant once (it had to do with religion), it has a lighter and more casual connotation today. To such an extent, mind you, that I regard a film made in France in 1933, (*Don Quixote*, by G.W. Pabst, starring Feodor Chaliapin in the title role and George Robey as Sancho Panza in the English version shown here) as the "godfather" of my daughter, Gretchen, born a decade later. I know I will have to explain this . . . ergo:

Talk about "lighter and more casual connotations" — what could be "lighter"* and "more casual" than to fall for (I don't really mean "fall" but it's a convenient slang term for it) a little chit of a girl, still in her teens, pretty but without a dime, working for me as a theatre usherette, as Erna did. And to follow Erna when that broke up, not long after, with falling (there's that word again) for yet another little chit of a girl, hardly out of her teens, again pretty and still without a dime, and, believe it or not, again working for me as a theatre usherette (at the 55th St. Playhouse, this time, one of the first of the little "art cinemas" in New York in the late Twenties, specializing in foreign films) and, as you've probably guessed by now, whom I also married.

Her name was Etta and she was from Odessa, in the Ukraine. (Erna was from Latvia, Windau on the coast — she had a brother, the fellow with the abacus). I can't say I learned about women from them because I'm as naive as I ever was on that complex subject but I had a full measure of "Slavic " temperament, between them, North and South variety. Etta was an only child — she came here very young with her parents from the Moldavankha district in the Caspian port city, the Jewish quarter. (Erna was a "shiksa — gentile girl — and had travelled alone to America by way of Danzig, German having become her second language.)

From the ghetto of Odessa to "Strunsky's Stables" in New

---

*Which reminds me of what a friend of Proust, the Comte Thierry de Montesquieu, vice-president of the Jockey Club in Paris, said after he'd been run over by two well known cocottes in their pony carriage, "Thank God, they were very light ladies!"

The author (1936) (Photo by Alfredo Valente)

York (bordering Washington Square South, Sullivan, Mac-
Dougal and West Third Streets, I think of Samuel Roth's
description of it —

What to me are boulevard, Charing Cross and
Wilhelmstrasse
Against Essex, Ludlow, Willet, Suffolk,
Lewis, Broome, Delancey, Norfolk —
Names that from my memory won't pass.)

—wasn't such a big hop for her. In no time she learned about
them and the block of tenements they comprised which were
let out to impecunious artists, would-be artists and non-artists,
so long as they needed shelter. Whether they could pay was
beside the point. Many Villagers in those days owed their sur-
vival to Mr. Strunsky. Her first job, prior to a brief stint as an
artist's model for the painter, Norman Rabinowitz, son of
Sholom Aleichem, as usherette at the then classy 55th St.
Playhouse uptown, where I met her, enabled her to find a
small furnished place of her own in the Chelsea district in the
West Twenties. A studio couch over which hung a batik on the
wall, table and a couple of chairs provided the furnishings. She
never owned a thing save her clothes, and these were of the
barest essentials. She hardly ever had any money after she paid
her rent but the unique thing about her which I discovered im-
mediately was that she was utterly incapable of a calculated ac-
tion. This quality was as rare as it was hazardous and I was
charmed by it, to put it mildly. Enraptured, would be closer.
For one who lived so precariously, she laughed a lot and was
given to spouting such self-made homilies as "I'll hitch a star to
my wagon, the better to light my way." She also had no small
talk which I noticed when I took her to a cocktail party. She
had nothing to say except when spoken to. She also never used
her hands in speaking, I noticed, and I liked that. There was
nothing fake about her. I found this astonishing for I took
fakery to be as much a part of the average person's make-up as
breathing. When I told her that her eyes were pretty and that
it was that about her which attracted me, she burst out with
the old gypsy love song, in Russian:

Otchi tchornia, otchi strassniya,
Otchi zhgootchiaya, yi prekrassniya,

Kak loobloo ya vas, kak boyoos ya vas,
Znat uvidiel vas, y v'nie debrychas!

There is no English that will do justice to it.

When I told her there was a restaurant in China called "The Restaurant of the Complete Amalgam of Virtues" to which I would have liked to take her, she said she was hungry and let's eat, which we did. While I watched her she looked up briefly just to say, "Aren't you eating?" I said I couldn't, I was too entranced with her to do such a prosaic thing. "There's nothing prosaic about eating," she said and went on.

She sang a lot. Another time she burst out with:

> *Mother, may I go out dancing?*
> *Yes my darling daughter.*
> *Mother may I try romancing?*
> *Yes my darling daughter.*
> *Mother, what if there's a moon above,*
> *Mother, what if he should talk of love,*
> *Mother must I keep on dancing?*
> *Yes, my darling daughter.*

Whereupon she immediately followed with the original Yiddish words, for the melody is a Yiddish one.

Another of her favorites, especially when the Andrews Sisters were singing it, was to join them in:

> *Bei mir bist du schön,*
> *Again I'll explain,*
> *It means that my heart's at your command!*
> *I could say "Bella, Bella," even "wunderbar,"*
> *Each language only helps me tell you how*
> > *grand you are*

at which moment the clarinet would spiral madly up to a wail for

> *I've tried to explain*
> *Bei mir bist du schon*
> *So kiss me and say you understand!*

Following which she'd go into the original Yiddish lyrics for this one, too, and end up in my arms.

What do you do with someone like that?

Once we passed the New York Foundling Home on Lexington Avenue with the plaque on its facade, "To the memory of Fritz and Harriet Kreisler." She wanted to go in. "It's a sad place," I told her, "orphans waiting for adoption." "I want to go in," she insisted, so we went in. They stood up in their cribs, their eyes following her. When we got down in the lobby, she could contain herself no longer. "I want one of my own," she

Etta and the author in Central Park, New York, summer of 1937

whimpered. "A little girl!" Then, "Oh, the poor dears up there! Without anyone to love them! It's really a wretched world!"

I took her to the press preview of *Gone With the Wind* at the Astor Theatre. The place was packed but we had seats up front. The picture had scarcely been on a few minutes when she suddenly said, "I'm going." "What do you mean, you're going?" I said. "Why? Don't you feel well?" "I feel fine," she said, "but I'll feel even finer if I get some fresh air." "But the picture's just started, you can't leave now." "Who says I can't?" she said, getting up. And we were being shushed all around. "This is an important press preview, *you can't do this,*" I said. But she was already half up the aisle with me after her. "What's the matter?" asked a solicitous MGM official behind the back row. "Is she ill?" How could I tell him that the picture bored her stiff after such a little while? I didn't even try. "She'll be alright," I said, "if she gets some fresh air." They made way for her and we got out. In the cab home she put her head on my shoulder and went to sleep. Blessed sleep. It may be that she was the only person who ever walked out on *Gone With the Wind,* which subsequently proved to be the most popular film in the whole history of American movies.

Years later Helen Lawrenson (who achieved a kind of immortality with *Latins Are Lousy Lovers,* was to refer to *Gone With the Wind* in her erotic fireworks pin-wheel of an autobiography *Whistling Girl,* as that "sappy soap opera." I don't think anybody was ever righter. Who was it — Mencken? — who said "Nobody ever lost money underestimating the American public." *Gone With the Wind,* as everyone knows, made a fortune.

When I came up from Baltimore in 1936, I stayed at the Paramount Hotel, following which I had a place at the London Terrace. Although still living in Chelsea, she often stayed overnight at the Terrace with me and one morning I found her preparing breakfast with just an open light robe of mine over her nakedness. "It isn't everyone gets a floorshow with his breakfast," she said.

I checked into the Barbizon-Plaza with her for a weekend before moving back to the Paramount. "A bash with class," we called it. "How'll I sign the register?" I asked her. "Mr. & Mrs. Smith?" "No," she said, "Mr. & Mrs. Wellington — since I'm your Waterloo." Which is how we signed in, after which I understood why so many streets in the British Empire were named Wellington, after what happened to Napoleon at Waterloo.

Once when I was going over some personal financial figures, she bent over to see, then said, in Yiddish, "Du virst sach oisrechnen." (You'll count yourself out yet.) Or she'd show me her epitaph:

Ode to a Grecian Urn

> *Herein the mortal ash of Etta*
> *And this is true, be it so known:*
> *There's no use denying that*
> *Only a man can keep her down.*

But it wasn't all facetious—she could spring from humorous verse to serious essays such as she did for *Sight & Sound*, official organ of the British Film Institute. One on social criticism was called "The Importance of Getting Angry."

Or we'd have a conversation like:

She: *Just think, she'd have my looks and your brains! Well, they're not so much, your brains, I mean, but it'll have to do, I'm afraid.*

Me: *Yes, but suppose she has . . .*

She: *I know—suppose she has your looks and my brains—like Shaw told Isadora Duncan ("My looks and your brains")—? Don't worry—she'll be a pretty girl. I know what I know.*

Me: *How do you know that?*

She: *How could she be anything but a girl, and a pretty one, since my mind's made up on it?*

Me: *But how do you know it'll be—?*

She: *Don't you call my little darling an "it"!*

Me: *I mean . . .*

She: *Of course she'll be a girl—mothers know things like that.*

Me: *But you're not a mother—yet.*

She: *I am when I think mother things.*

And so on.

My life was full of irony in those days. Erna and I were married by a Baltimore rabbi and Etta and I in a civil ceremony at the marriage license bureau in New York's Municipal Building, with its admonishments and dire warnings in the form of scrawled graffiti by my predecessors all over the place, wherever there was a blank space, a wall, a blotter, anywhere:

Etta (1944) "Forever wilt thou love and she be fair" (Photo by Dan Dugger)

"Wait! Are you sure you know what you're doing? Think it Over! He who falls in love has come to the end of happiness." and similar homilies. Etta smiled at them and urged me to consider them even if it meant reconsidering the "fatal step" I was about to take. "It's your last chance," she said, and I looked up from the form I was filling out and exchanged smiles with her, slowly shaking my head. *"You're* my last chance," I said. Thirty-four years later, as I write this, I realize how right I was, for a year later Gretchen was born to us.

We come now to the point of all this, which took place on the eve of Gretchen's appearance the next morning. It was past midnight when I was flagging every taxi that passed to stop and take us to the hospital. None stopped, all were occupied, and I was desperate. I went out into the street, determined to wave to a halt any car coming, taxi or no taxi, and plead with them to take us. The first car that came along, grinding to an abrupt stop to prevent running into me, was a taxi and when I ran to the door to make my plea I recognized an old friend—good old Valdemar Bell, a "White" Russian refugee who fled the Communists with his wife by way of Paris, where he picked up a film to distribute here while she opened a ballet school on 56th St. between 6th and 7th Avenues, that odd little street devoted to garages and music. Well, what more need I tell you? "Of course!" he said, getting out of the cab. Etta rushed in, with me following. "I'll never forget you for this!" I shouted to him as the cab got under way (Etta having already told the driver where to go) and I remember Valdemar shouting back, "Good luck—and a big kiss!" I took her hand. "We're in luck," I said, "it's a good start, a happy omen—everything's going to be all right . . . "

Well, yes, what I have to tell you to bring this anecdote to full circle, is that the film that brought Valdemar to New York was, of course, Pabst's *Don Quixote,* which Paul Morand, my favorite French writer, had adapted from Cervantes, and ever since which it has been my "pet" of all favorite films, and I never miss a chance to see it, not only because it reminds me of that night but because it is also a perfectly charming film. For the record, it was the night of May 16, 1943.

I was up all night, smoking away, till nigh onto the morning of the 17th, when the nurse wheeled a crib out into the corridor and said to the infant in it, "Say hello to your father." Not a sound. "Come on," said the nurse, giving the infant's cheek a few quick pats to wake the child. This time a brief cry was emitted and back to sleep the child went. "What is it?" I asked, quite beside myself. "What do you mean 'it'?" said the nurse. "She's going to be a beautiful child." "I knew it," I murmured to myself. *I knew it*—she *had* to be a little girl! "Thank you," I said, as I bent over to kiss her cheek. Her first kiss—from her father, her first beau. "Thank you for being a little girl." The nurse smiled and wheeled her away.

I went out for coffee and came refreshed by the morning mist. I took the light drizzle as an omen of happiness (I was to learn that there is something to that—to rain as a good omen) and went back to see Etta. She had her baby with her, and seemed to be counting the child's toes "What are you doing?" I said. "I don't want anymore than I'm entitled to; but neither will I take any less," she said. "I want a fair shake . . . 8-9-10." Then she began on other aspects of the child. "Two ears, two eyes, one nose, no teeth yet . . . " When she got to the child's fingers she ended with "9, 10, 11 . . . oh, my goodness!" And started counting again, ending this time with "8, 9, 10 . . . oh, thank goodness!" Then turning to me, "Go away, you're mixing me all up. Besides, I'm tired." And with her arm around the babe, she turned away and went to sleep. I left them both sleeping . . . blessed sleep.

"When we love," said Walter Benjamin, "our existence runs through nature's fingers like golden coins that she cannot hold and lets fall to purchase new birth thereby."

Some months afterward, having taken a nurse for Gretchen, we thought we'd take a weekend off and go to Atlantic City. We returned late Sunday night and found the baby asleep and the nurse reading. Our conversation must have wakened the child for she was soon standing in her crib holding on to the side, and, in stentorian tones, seemed to be admonishing us. What came out sounded like:

"Splotchiyama gohan daya ingalook awiawhollok ngta!"

"What did she say?" I asked Etta. She had long ago assured me that she could understand baby gibberish—all mothers could, she said, even though it remained a mystery to fathers.

"She said what did we mean by leaving her alone a whole weekend with a stranger."

"Anna is no stranger," I said wearily, "She's been her nurse for the last six months."

The child went on and Etta translated . . .

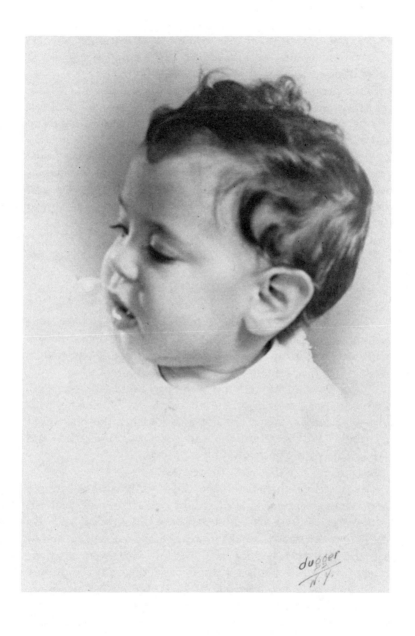

Gretchen at 10 months (1944) (Photo by Dan Dugger)

"She says anyone other than you or me is a stranger to her."

Etta went to her, embraced her and assured her it would never happen again.

Came the day when she was to enter the Ecole Française du St. Esprit, a pre-school kindergarten. A bus, already half full of kids, had pulled up in front of our house and although we had been preparing Gretchen for weeks for this day she held on for dear life to her mother and wouldn't let go. Somehow she must have been inveigled by Etta to get on the bus for she was placed by her on a window seat, given a big hug and a kiss and then left there as Etta returned from the bus. No sooner did Gretchen see her back with me again she started to cry.

"Oh, dear," I said. "Now look at her!"

"Let her alone," said Etta, "She'll get over it, there's a first time for everything."

You would have to have a heart of stone to resist such tears, I felt.

"She's crying because she thinks this will make us come rushing to her and take her off that god-damned bus that's going to take her away from her mommy and daddy whom she's never going to see again," I said, all in one breath too.

"We've been all through this with her," said Etta, "She'll get used to it, you'll see." And she ran over to her outside her window seat, blew a kiss up to her and told her the bus would bring her back that afternoon and not to worry — she would have a fine time at school.

As, indeed, she did, as it turned out.

I even visited the school one day shortly afterwards. No sooner had I entered the classroom when they all scurried around me, Gretchen pushing her way through, saying, "Go away, he's my daddy." I sat down and she sat herself on my lap, the kids surrounding us. After all, they were all first-timers, too, and I was a welcome visitation from the outside world that they, too, must have reluctantly left behind.

"As you can see," said the teacher afterwards to me, "this won't do. It upsets the other children, whose parents haven't come to take them on their knee. You understand, I'm sure."

"Of course," I said. Of course.

I have charming souvenirs that Gretchen brought home from the school—drawings, scrawls that would have enchanted Paul Klee, twirls and whirligigs that would have enchanted Picasso who once said, upon seeing a folio of children's drawings, "It took me thirty years to learn to draw like that."

Memories . . . Memories . . . of happy days that followed. We lived on an edge of Central Park, right off Fifth Avenue, on East 89th St., around the corner from the future Guggenheim Museum, and Gretchen practically grew up in the park. Jolly days taking pictures in the park (I documented almost every week of her life since her birth in snapshots), lolling on the grass—she, her mother and I—playing in sandboxes or climbing a jungle-gym or going down the chutes, bicycling, row-boating on the lake, sailng little sailboats on the lake, taking pony-cart rides, making the rounds of all the pet animals in the zoo, lunching at the cafeteria in the zoo. I even bought her, at the F.A.O. Schwarz toy store, that veritable heaven of toys for children, a full-size sled for her there, looking like the kind the boy Czarevich must have been driven in during the long Russian winters.

I have a snapshot of Gretchen in her carriage, when still a babe, smiling in her sleep. Dreaming of fountains or whatever is the equivalent for a 10-months-old of ice cream sodas? What teaches a child to smile? Or to recognize for the first time a smile on the face of its mother? The commonest of occurrences never ceases to be the most wonderful, as full of mystery as the mystery of birth itself . . .

Yes, memories . . . I once said before, if it were not for memories, who could say that we had lived? The problems of burping after taking in so much formula in her bottle (that elixir of condensed milk and dextrose) with such relish that a lot of air bubbles went in with it, the result being a glazed look in the child's eyes, as if she no longer saw us. The idea was to expel those bubbles. "Come on, baby," I'd say, walking up and down the room with her in my arms, "give mommy and daddy a nice big burp." Some times it took a while but when it came, with its attendant grin on her face from ear to ear, it was a sight to see. There was also the time when I walked what seemed half the night with her in my arms when she had fever, or the time when she described a perfect arc or parabola when she flew off on the up-swing of a see-saw that I was manipulating for her and landed with a thud on the ground. I steeled myself in the brief moment of awful silence that followed for what I knew was coming—a yell to shiver one's timbers. In a taxi to her pediatrician to have x-rays taken. "Don't worry," the doctor said, "at that age they're made of rubber—they bounce, they don't break. To a degree, it's a matter of cartilage rather than bone at her age." Then he smiled and concluded, "And besides, up to a certain point, children are in a state of grace. Of course, the thing is—you never know when you've exceeded that point. It's a deep dark mystery, known only to children and God, so you'd better be careful." He was right. The x-ray was "clean as a whistle" but, all the same, we treated see-saws gingerly from then on. Dolls and stuffed animals, a whole menagerie of them, but mostly stuffed animals to engender a love for the real animals she saw in the zoo. Her favorite was the giraffe. Years later she would take up one of the giraffes, whom she called Florian, (we must have had a dozen giraffes) and bring him to life with a humorous dialogue she had with him, not only humorous but witty. About this time she also ventured into verse and one of her first was "Snow" at the age of nine. In class the kids were to write about the snow which was lying thick on the street outside and falling past the classroom windows. The teacher corrected her punctuation:

> The snow is falling all around,
>   whitely, whitely;
> It covers every tree in town,
>   lightly, lightly.
> Down it comes, down it comes,
>   softly, softly;
> Soft as feathers, soft as down,
>   quickly, quickly.

In return for which, I told her, I would do a sheaf of poems for her:

CHILDREN'S GAMES

> Bounce the ball,
>   sweep up the jacks
> And catch the ball again . . .
>
> I will hide
>   and you will seek,
> But not till I say when . . .

One
two-three
and
hop and scotch,
seven
eight-nine
and
ten . . .

Turn around
and
hop you go,
all the way back
again.

ON THE BEACH
The breakers roar
on the wide bright strand,
The waves wash over
the glistening sand,
And a child's bare feet
makes prints where she stands,
And like star-fish hover
the pretty child's hands.

THE TRAPPED FOX
The trap springs closed
on the young fox's foot
And he sniffs the cold steel
wondering why, wondering why . . .
And he listens to the crunch
of the distant boot
Coming closer, coming closer,
Wondering why, wondering why . . .

(She said she didn' like the last one because it was too sad.)

Years later, when, still in her teens, she was on an Oscar Wilde kick (we must have had every book there was on him), I told her about Wilde's claiming that he had written the world's shortest short story (didn't he claim it was the greatest, too?) (Christ's encounter with three men who were formerly blind, crippled and dead, and who were now no longer so, thanks to him.)

"Well," I said, "I've written one even shorter, tho' I don't say it's better. It's called *The First Story . . .*"

Adam, in the Garden of Eden, watches, for the first time, the setting sun. He is apprehensive. When it disappears and grows dark he weeps. Exhausted from weeping he falls asleep. The next morning he wakes to find the sun high in the heavens. A smile breaks out on his face for now he knows it will always be like that. (The first fear, the first tears, the first sleep, and the first smile.)

* * *

It was the early Thirties. I'd been busy titling foreign films into English subtitles for American audiences, since 1929. It had marked a turning point for me as, previous to that, I'd been studying the violin at the Institute of Musical Art in New York, forerunner of the Juilliard School, when Frank Damrosch (brother of Walter) was running it. After an audition I was assigned to Louis Svecenski, viola player in the Kneisel Quartet. Kneisel was first fiddler of the quartet and head of the school's violin department. I didn't make his class but to study with Svecenski was considered a close second. I began with Kreutzer and got up to the Mendelssohn Concerto when I met Richard Watts, then film editor of The New York Herald-Tribune — the year was 1927 — and he invited me to write for his Sunday movie page. "I get a lot of canned stuff from the studios," he opined, "and I'm looking for outside original material." "What'll I write about?" I asked. "Anything so long as it's even remotely connected with the movies," he said. That did it. A three part article by me that appeared on three successive Sundays on the new art that had sprung up in the era of silent movies — the arranging and composing of original music for motion pictures, sometimes by famous composers like Saint-Saëns, Honegger, Georges Auric, Darius Milhaud, Edmund Meisel, Hans Eisler, etc., sometimes by Victor Herbert and Sigmund Romberg (did you know Romberg wrote the original score for the premiere of Stroheim's *Foolish Wives?*) and such arrangers as James Bradford *(Greed)*, David Mendoza and William Axt *(The Big Parade)*, Hugo Reisenfeld *(Tabu, Thunder Over Mexico)*, etc. The day after the last of the three articles appeared I received a telegram from the 5th Avenue Playhouse (66 Fifth Avenue) asking me if I'd like a job. I was all of 19 then and flattered no end at the request. My first job. I left the conservatory (never to return) and took what turned out for me to be "the easiest way." (Like the girls in a thousand anecdotes who also took "the easiest way," I used to say, explaining my shift.) It was certainly easier than studying to possibly become a concert violinist. The fiddle is a damned difficult instrument to play well and who could play like Heifetz? ("Malkin" — who was Heifetz's teacher before Auer in St. Petersburg — "Malkin should hear him now!" I overheard Rivkin Heifetz, the violinist's father, say in back of the last row at Carnegie Hall one afternoon, during an intermission.) Heifetz must have broken a thousand fiddlers' hearts — like he broke mine. What was the use? We gave up — and took an easier way — and left it all to him. If God created the world, that was his thing. If Heifetz played as seraphically as he did, that was his thing. Why compete with people like that? That's the kind of a tizzy Heifetz threw all aspiring violinists into. And that's how I surrendered and rejoined the rest of the human race. In the movies I began as a writer of glossy articles (I was told I had a "flair" for that) and since I had now grown to like movies (after that first *Foolish Wives* en-counter) I was in a way something like the *demi-mondaine* in the Molnar anecdote who when asked how she became so suc-cessful as a *fille de joie*, answered, *"Mon Dieu! Que voulez-vous?* It was like with you, *mon chou,* I adored love-making like you adored writing — and when I found that people would pay for it — What could be better?" I liked movies, especially the foreign ones I was engaged to work on — from France, Germany, Russia — and when I found out that people would pay me for writing about them — what indeed could be better?

All of which is by the way of prelude to what happened next. Someone with nothing better to do one day discovered the principle of the photo-electric cell which made it possible to transmit soundwaves into light waves and vice-versa, and which now made it possible for movies to talk. But when the films I was working with talked it was in French and German. What do we do now? Full screen titles was the first answer, stopping the action and giving the audience a brief synopsis of what they were going to see in the next ten minutes. Ten minutes later, another full-screen synopsis. This was not only silly but annoying as those in the audience who could under-stand the language could laugh at the jokes in between the full screen titles while those who couldn't (and they constituted the majority, by far) sat there glum, doubly irritated by the laughter of the linguists in the house. Obviously something had to be done to placate the customers before they started asking for their money back. Then someone discovered the existence of a mechanism called a "moviola." It had been used for years in editing films. It was like a miniature projection room. You could start and stop the film at will. It had a counter which enabled you to measure every piece of dialogue because it, too, was now equipped with that magical photo-electric cell so that you could now measure not only the length of every scene but that of every line of dialogue. And from these measurements we were able, by the trial and error-method (until the rules of how many words in a subtitle on the bottom of the screen could be read in the time it took the actors to say anywhere from two to three times that many words, could be formulated) to determine what we were doing and why. Whew! And when I say "we" I mean *me*, as no one knew any more than anyone else did about it and I seemed to be the only one willing to go ahead with the actual writing and make something out of it.

At the beginning I was very cautious and superimposed hardly more than 25 or 30 titles to a ten-minute reel (the average film ran from 80 to 90 minutes). Then I'd go into the theatre during a showing to watch the audiences' faces, to see how they reacted to the titles. I'd wondered if they were going to drop their heads slightly to read the titles at the bottom of the screen and then raise them again after they read the titles (like watching a tennis match and moving your head from left to right and back again) but I needn't have worried on this score; they didn't drop their heads, they merely dropped their eyes, I noticed. This emboldened me to insert more titles, when warranted, of course, and bit by bit more and more of the original dialogue got translated until at the end of my work in this field I was putting in anywhere from 100 to 150 titles a reel . . . tho', I must repeat, only when the dialogue was good enough to warrant it — as in films like *Grand Illusion*, the *Marius-Fanny-Cesar* trilogy of Marcel Pagnol, *Open City* and *Shoe Shine*, *The Four Hundred Blows*, *Forbidden Games*, *Paisan*, *La Strada*, *Maedchen in Uniform*, *The Three-Penny-Opera* . . . Altogether I did some 400 films between 1929 and a few years ago. My last was *The Little Theatre of Jean Renoir*. I used to tell the students in my class at the City College where I taught a course in film history and aesthetics between 1960 and 1976: "If you want to see and hear two 'swan songs' for the price of one, see *The Little Theatre of Jean Renoir* — it's not only Renoir's last film as a director but also mine as a writer of English subtitles."

Of course, there were other problems — censorship for one. They were very strict in the pre-permissive period. Strict and stupid and frequently I was called on to do my best to save a scene or a fragment of dialogue in the titles, when cuts were demanded, usually on the grounds of "obscenity" etc. I could cite a score of cases (especially where French and Italian films, with their racy dialogue was concerned — the Latin languages are particularly colorful, exploding with expletives for which literal translations would never do — an *equivalent* in English had to be found — and sometimes I went far away, tho' never far amiss, if I say so myself, to find it).

Whenever I worked with a language which was completely foreign to me—like Urdu, Japanese, Greek or Czech—I always had at my side one whose native language it was, but the final English version, with regard to nuance (as important as meaning, and never forget it!) as well as meaning was my own. Since I was prepared to take the rap for it, no one else's English was going to serve but my own—and English was one language I felt fully "at home" in.

I sometimes would, when nothing else could be done, agree to eliminate the title to save the dialogue and the scene that went with it. That is, the censors would let the scene stay in, with its racy dialogue, if it wasn't translated—probably feeling that those who understood the racy original were already too far gone to save. As for the so-called "four-letter words," often met with full strength in English titles on the screens today, in the 400 films I titled I used such a word only once, in the Italian film, *The Organizer* (with Marcello Mastroiani), and it was really one of the harmless ones (i.e., harmless to one's sensibilities) and it fitted so rightly that I couldn't resist using it. It was the English for *merde*. That's a far cry from such foul debasement of the English language as was exploited in the American film, *Slap Shot,* or from the gratuitous all-but-unbelievable scabrous "bomb-shells" of *Shampoo.* The stupidity of the censorship boards (in New York by a division of the State Board of Education, no less) was even at its worst not to be construed as an excuse for the demeaning of both language and sensibilities on the screen today ever since the Supreme Court, in one of its most dubious judgments, wrapped pornography in the hallowed folds of the First Amendment to our poor, battered good old Constitution, giving films like *Slap Shot* and *Shampoo* (not to mention the rest of the offal) the protection of "Free Speech."

Still, I must give you at least one example of what I mean by what constituted a characteristic instance of the stupidity of film censorship in those "good old days." (Tho' I'm not kidding about the "good, old days." I could draw up a list of films produced under censorship then that would read like a Roll of Honor of cinema achievement and I defy anyone to match it with a comparable list in films produced since the bars of censorship were let down. So, the lack of censorship hasn't freed the screen to do better work than it could ever have done before—not by a long shot, *Slap Shot*.)

Well, then, it happened at the Maryland State Board of Motion Picture Censors. I'd been asked by the American distributors of the Swedish film, *Miss Julie* (from the Strindberg play) which I'd titled, to save some cuts they wanted to make in it, particularly one where Miss Julie says to her father's valet who has been laying her, "You're not going to marry me? You expect me to continue like this, as your concubine?" They objected to the word, "concubine." When I couldn't understand their objection (the censors were three middle-aged ladies acting under a chairman of the board) saying that it was a good old biblical word, etc., they remonstrated, "But the modern connotation of the word is entirely different." "How is it different?" I asked. "Well," said the spokesman of the trio, in her haughtiest accents. "Everyone knows that the modern connotation of a concubine is that of a white woman living with a Chinaman." Talk about "racism"! Anyway, the phenomenon here was that she was remembering all the lurid paperbacks about the "yellow peril," not forgetting the role Hearst's newspapers, like The Sunday New York American, played with stuff like that in their weekend magazine supplements—tales of white women trapped into sliding down shutes in some out-of-the-way twist in a street in a Chinatown, here or in London's Soho, or some such place, and finding themselves in an opium den or worse (the ubiquitous white-slave "clearing house"), etc. Such women became the "concubines" in due course of their Chinese masters.* The censor-board's spokeswoman had a

*In Old San Francisco, with Anna May Wong and So Jin was one such Hollywood film.

head-full of such fantasies. Of course, any good psychiatrist (remembering what Freud said that "the greater the attraction, the greater the repression") would have diagnosed her case immediately and recommended — as delicately as possible, of course — that what she was in sore need of was "some sex," not necessarily with a Chinaman — any virile young man would do — and not only would she be a happier woman but, as a result, the world would be a happier place. To make this already too long re-telling shorter, when I reported what she said to the chairman, he smiled and said that it would do no harm, in this case, to overrule her, which he did. (I didn't tell him about the psychiatrist because I didn't want him to think I was impudent, certainly not on the heels of a victory, which could be reversed in an instant, I was certain, but I knew I'd probably be back here in a while on another case and I'd best not "pull the lion's beard in his own den." (Is that saying it right?) (Not long after that, they really crucified the Czech film, *Ecstasy*, the famous one with Hedy Lamarr (when she was still Hedy Kiesler). But that, too, is another story.)

This is the way it was with film censorship when it was rampant here. This is why it was knocked out by the courts, because of its stupid application. Eventually it was ruled unconstitutional by the U.S. Supreme Court, "being in violation of the First Amendment because the screen merited the same freedom of speech that other media enjoyed." And so, as a result of this nonsense (I mean the way censorship was applied, not the Supreme Court decision, though that turned out to be even worse than nonsense), the censors so infuriated the film distributors that the latter took the matter to the courts, claiming the guarantees of Free Speech, etc. . . and the Supreme Court sustained them. Now we have a "free screen," which is to say a screen enslaved by the cupidity of its entrepreneurs (Ironic, no, that the word "cupidity" should have the ancient Roman god of love "Cupid," son of Venus, as its heart, considering with what greed they exploited the *grande passion?*) — the same entrepreneurs who were so vocal and full of righteous indignation as a cover-up for their greed in shouting down censorship. So where we once were charmed by screen subtlety in matters of sex by Lubitsch and his followers we now wallow in the autopsy or atrocity to our sensibilities in works by Robert Altman, Bertolucci (I think of *The Wedding, Last Tango of Paris,* and *Luna*) and their followers. I won't even mention the license it gave to the pornographers and their like.

1942 . . .

And then it came — "Greetings" from Uncle Sam . . .

We were deep in World War II by then and my draft board had finally caught up with me (of all times, now that I'd started a family!) Without telling Etta, I went to the board's headquarters in the Hotel Roosevelt where the grand ballroom on the mezzanine floor had been converted into a clearing house where all data on draftees, deferments, etc. were collated and filed. I filled out a form with a sinking heart and saw it countersigned, stamped, processed in sixteen different ways and was finally handed a card denoting my draft status. They ranged from A-1 to 4-F. In normal times if you were ranked A-1 in anything that meant the best. This time it was the worst — meaning you were in perfect condition to be drafted into the armed services, a polite way of saying you were fit to get your head blown off in some foreign clime. The succeeding weeks were among the darkest hours of my life. And when I read one morning that the director of my draftboard had destroyed all his files so that no record of anyone remained in that particular clearing station, I blessed him in my heart's core deeper than I had ever blessed anyone or anything in my life. The poor fellow, after having done his "bit" to protest the idiocy of war and the criminality of sending young men to die for its filthy cause, had shot himself.

Still, I applied to the Joint Chiefs of Staff that year and received a reply from the Office of the Coordinator of Government Films saying I might be called in due course, thanking me for offering my services, etc. I never heard further and they won the war without me.

Of course there were the Nazis and somebody, somehow, had to stop them but why did the world let it happen? Where was reason? Where for that matter was God? *Was* there a God? If so — how then could it have happened? Churchill's "V" for "Victory" signs were no help, though none were more valiant than the English. Men died while he was waving his "Victory" signs and smoking his cigars. Of course he meant well — everybody meant well — and still men died. The other horrors need no naming from me. After Hiroshima, when peace finally came, and Etta broke down and wept with relief as so many others must have wept, the night the late papers announced the Japanese surrender and the end of the war, I was on Times Square. Nothing like it will ever happen again, I'm sure. For if there is ever another war, from the technological advances they learned from the last one, there'll be no such old fashioned thing anymore as a formal surrender and symbolic breaking of swords over the knee or whatever hocus-pocus they employed with a straight face to placate the populace back home in the "surrender rituals for murdering their sons . . . " Whatever it will be, it won't be a pretty sight, if there'll be anything left to see at all, let alone soldiers and sailors kissing the girls on Times Square that night as they must have been kissing in London, Paris, Rome . . . What did they do in the rubble of Dresden, Berlin or Tokyo?

God moves in mysterious ways,
His wonders to perform;
He plants his footsteps in the sea,
And rides upon the storm . .

        . . . wrote Cowper . . .

Blind unbelief is sure to err,
And scan his work in vain;
God is his own interpreter,
And he will make it plain.
Yup, as Gary Cooper used to say.

We celebrated Gretchen's 5th birthday with a gala party. Everyone in town I knew who wasn't away seemed to be there—the German film producer, Max Glass, Tom Curtiss, Klaus Mann, Valdemar Bell (of course), Irene Thirer, film critic of the New York Post, Hans Richter, Fritz Lang among them—and Etta entertained by singing some of her songs to the accompaniment of a friend's piano-accordion. The one I remember most was

Take me in your arms,
Before you take your love away,
Take me in your arms
Before we part . . .
Let me thrill again
To your caress of yesterday,
Let me fill again
My hungry heart . . .

Times Square at night (1947) (New York Public Library — Picture Collection)

A night at the Stork Club the author attended when Deems Taylor, Barry Fitzgerald and George Jean Nathan were also there. (1955) (Collection of the author)

> *One hour of gladness*
> *That we knew in the past*
> *One moment's madness*
> *Although it be the last—hold fast—*
> *Blind me with your charms*
> *With all the star-dust in the sky,*
> *Take me in your arms*
> *And then goodbye . . .*

One of the imperishable love songs of the Thirties which she made her very own whenever she sang it and which always moved me whenever I heard her sing it. And then she was stricken . . cancer of the liver—inoperable then, operable to-day . . .

One night I visited her in the hospital after dinner and she was up. We walked the length of the hospital hallway while I supported her. I took it as a good sign that she could walk, she even joked, and I was sure she was making real progress. When we got back to her room, she said she'd like a mint-julep—she'd never had one, she said. Great, I thought. I joyously brought one up for her from the bar across the street, but when I offered it to her in bed she shook her head and pleaded, "I want to see my baby . . . " I told her I'd bring Gretchen tomorrow. Then she closed her eyes and turned her head away. I sat at her bedside holding her hand, her cold hand, while the world continued to turn on its blasted axis, and then, after a long while—how long was it—a minute, an hour?—she parted her lips and began to sing . . . that strange and terrible moment when she began to sing with what little remained of her voice, once so full-throated and now, with all but no voice at all, she began to sing, but she heard it, to her it was the old song she had loved so and I heard it . . . even if no one else could have made it out . . .

> *Take me in your arms*
> *Before you take your love away,*
> *Take me in your arms*
> *Before we part . . .*

A tear coursed slowly down her cheek, her lips trembled over the words of the song but now no sound came out . . . I looked into her eyes and she looked into mine, her lips still moving without a sound, her eyes desperately holding onto mine as if I could keep her from sinking farther and farther away from me, from life, from the world, from everything that ever happened since the creation of the universe . . . most of all from her baby whom I promised I would bring the next day . . . the next day . . . the next aeon . . .

This is the first time in some thirty years, since that night in 1950, that I have spoken, as I do now, about it. I never had—not even to Gretchen—and never will again. I will let those few lines of Emily Dickinson act as guardian over it . . . not that there's any consolation in it, she knew there's no consolation in it—still she said it . . .

> *The bustle in the house*
> *The morning after death*
> *Is solemnest of industries*
> *Enacted upon earth.*

> *The sweeping up the heart,*
> *And putting love away,*
> *We shall not want to use again*
> *Until eternity.*

She laughed a lot, sang her songs, gave birth to a child more beautiful than the cherubs of Raphael—and she died.

It was a time when if something like that happened a rush of memories would each hug for first place in you—like the one that echoed Conrad Aiken's

> *Music I heard with you*
> *   was more than music,*
> *And bread I broke with you*
> *   was more than bread . . .*

Remember?

How do you tell a child she will never see her mother again? There's no way . . .

Gretchen . . .

As a child, she never skipped. This is most unusual because all children (all little girls, that is) skip . . . that blithe skipping a step while walking, something like a one-footed hop . . . I took this as a good omen—that she'd be different from the average girl, that there'd be little or nothing that was "average" about her. I dreamt about it and what it could mean, what forms it could take . . .

We moved to West 71st St., again near a park—Riverside Park, this time.

In the months following the death of her mother, I told her bedtime stories every night and sang her to sleep with lullabies. The stories and lullabies were my own with the exception of *Sweet and Low*, after Tennyson.

The Tennyson one went:

> *Sweet and low, sweet and low,*
> *Wind of the western seas . . .*
> *Low, low, breathe and blow,*
> *Wind of the western seas . . .*
> *Daddy will come to his babe in the nest,*
> *Silver sails all all out of west,*
> *Blow him right back to me,*
> *Sleep my little one, sleep my pretty one,*
> *Sleep . . .*

Gretchen was six when bereft of her mother. I brought her up for the next twelve years. If anyone were to tell me I'd do this one day, I'd have said he was balmy. Doesn't everyone have reserves of strength he doesn't know he has until called upon to use it? Especially if it is a matter of father and daughter?

"Help the girl orphan before the boy orphan, for the boy may beg, but not the girl," says the Talmud. But I recently saw a pretty girl begging on 6th Avenue and 58th Street (where I first lived with Gretchen and her mother) — the place where George Kaufman said he wanted to be every night at dusk. She sat on an abutment from the building there and asked passersby if they "could spare some change." What do you say to that, New York? Up the block a few steps and around the corner, men and their girls were sipping cocktails on the sidewalk terrace of the St. Moritz Hotel. Where were the parents of this girl? Did they know to what she was reduced? How rich is a world in which the adults are rich and the children are poor?

One day, I think she was about 7 or 8, I'd taken Gretchen along because I wanted to see *The Cabinet of Dr. Caligari* again. She didn't like it because it was too "scary" she said, so she wandered up the aisle and back until she stopped by my seat to tell me that there was a man standing behind the back row who said he wrote the film. "What do you mean, 'He wrote the film'?" I asked her. "That's what he said." "He told *you* that?" "Uhuh." Both Carl Mayer and Hans Janowitz, authors of the film, were dead, so how could anyone who says he wrote the film be standing back there telling idle stories like that? But I became curious and went back and met him. It was

Hans Janowitz, all right, and he wasn't dead, he was living in New York and was in the import-export business on West 42nd Street. He gave me his card. I promised to see him for an interview. But when I got around to it, I was informed by his office that he had just "passed away." I was too late. (Years later I saw a Noel Coward film with Robert Newton about middle-class English life.* The wife remarks on the fact that so-and-so had just "passed away," which irks her husband, Newton, into saying, "He didn't pass on, he didn't pass away, nor did he pass out — he just died."

We were arguing once about something and Gretchen said, at one point, "I'm *not* arguing. I just don't see the point of anything." That was at age 11.

When she was still little, and there were now just the two of us, I used to leave her, after breakfast each morning, in the children's room of the library at 5th Avenue and 42nd St. Then I went about my business and picked her up around 5 PM for dinner. When she grew up, I'd leave her at our place after breakfast and an "à bientôt" kiss. But one morning I forgot the kiss and when I came back I found her asleep but in the typewriter on the desk was a sheet of paper on which she'd typed a poem for me to read when I came in:

DON'T FORGET TO KISS GOODBYE
Don't forget to kiss goodbye,
No matter where you're going.
For that kiss will last a while,
And while the time is flowing,
The moist spot upon our cheek
Won't last a day, won't last a week,
It only lasts a minute, but
A minute of love's worth knowing.

Those were happy days—they had to be—I had to be not only father and mother, now, but now that she was growing up I had also to be what true dads invariably are, their daughter's first beau, too. That meant "grooming" her for her first real beau. Before she was sixteen she'd had a full complement of French, piano and ballet. Like her mother, she never used her hands in speaking, and still doesn't. An augury of things to

---

This Happy Breed (1944) David Lean, director, written produced by Noel Coward.

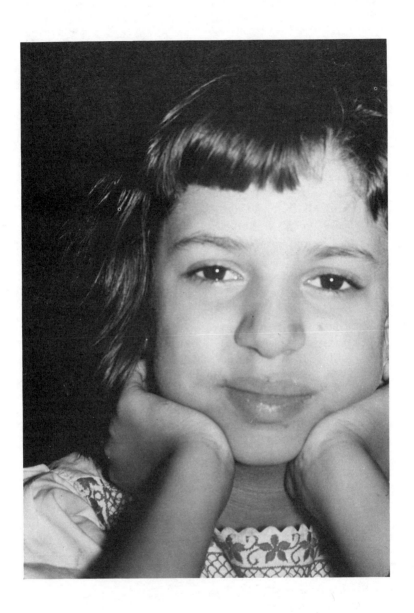

Gretchen (1950) (Photo by the author)

come (her talent as a writer was her joshing—she liked to play with words. "Is it called adultery," she asked one day with a perfectly straight face, "because adults commit it?" Or when I once mentioned the Polish singer, Jan Kiepura, she remarked, "That's the Jewish holiday, isn't it?")

She came back from the Professional Children's School one day (she was enrolled there with Jenny Hecht, Ben and Rose Hecht's daughter, with whom she was at one time close friends) and said she'd heard the kids there spouting a gag they'd made up about Christ. Their parents may have been devout church-goers and all that but they were like children all over the world—free of all shibboleths. On the road to Calvary, they reported, he was stopped by a Roman soldier who said to him, "I don't care who you are, this is a one-way street!" Grisly children's humor, but they were children of their time.

Gretchen had her own reflection about the Deity. "Everybody's intrigued by things they don't understand," she once said, "that's why God is so popular."

"Certain it is," wrote Sir Richard Steele in *The Spectator*, 1712, " . . . there is no kind of affection so pure and angelick as that of a father to a daughter. He beholds her both with and without regard to her sex. In love to our wives there is desire, to our sons there is ambition, but in that to our daughters, there is something for which there are no words to express. Her life is designed wholly domestic, and she is so ready a friend and companion, that everything that passes about a man is accompanied with the idea of her presence."

That's how it was with me and Gretchen.

One day she gave me a poem for my birthday . . . (1957— she was 14):

SUCH IS MY LOVE

Grass in the wind,
Moon in the trees,
Such is my love,
For you, like these.

Swaying clouds,
turbulent ocean,
Such is my love,
Like a bittersweet potion.

Falling star,
Swirling comet,
Crashing heavens, too.
Through all these,
My love comes down,
With a fiery tail,
For you.

High as a mountain,
Swift as a bird,
From my rock,
A song I heard.

Sweet and wild,
Rose and thorn,
Cry of the living,
The dying, the born.

Sky and water,
Wind and tree,
Take my love,
To go with thee!

And that Christmas, to show her gratitude to me for the little stuffed giraffe I gave her, the one she called Florian, and which was her favorite among her whole menagerie, the one she brought to life with humorous dialogue, her Christmas card to me had the following written on it:

TO DAD FOR CHRISTMAS

You gave me Florian, and then
In him you breathed life, I knew.
Whatever of him has left my ken
Goes homing back to you.
My gift is ready and comes to meet
The father it longs to see—
It would be my present to you, Daddy,
If it weren't your gift to me.

She was 16 that year. Sir Richard knew what he was saying.

After I was all but charmed out of my wits by it, she reminded me that she got it from A.A. Milne's "Winnie the Pooh," but "Nobody," I assured her, "ever said it better than you." And if ever I meant anything I meant exactly that.

Going over this with Gretchen recently, she said: "Beginning writers always steal things before going on to find their own voice."

I know a sunset shore
  Where warm keen incense on the sea-wind blows,
And dim blue ranches, while these March winds roar,
  Drown to the roofs in heliotrope and rose;

Deserts of lost delight,
  Cactus and palm and earth of thirsty gold,
Dark purple blooms round eaves of sun-washed white
  And that Hesperian fruit men sought of old . . .

All things come to those who wait—
  Palms against a deeper blue,
  Far Cathay and Zipangu,
And the Golden Gate.

Alfred Noyes

"Everyone who disappears, is said to have been seen in San Francisco. It must be a delightful place and possess all the attractions of the next world."

> —OSCAR WILDE, *The Picture of Dorian Gray.*

"San Francisco is a mad city inhabited by perfectly insane people whose women are of a remarkable beauty."

> —RUDYARD KIPLING

"New York is not only the youngest international metropolis; it is also the youngest American city, no matter what the arithmetic of chronology says. Cities like Houston and Los Angeles—if that vast scrambled settlement can be called a city—are not so much young as simply new. Chicago, having sown its wild oats, has come into respectable middle-age. And among New York's chronological age group, Boston is the *grande dame*, Philadelphia the fine old gentleman, and New Orleans the raddled old madam of American cities. (San Francisco is just San Francisco, beyond categorizing or characterizing.)

> —The New York Times

"I've never seen anything like it . . . it's as if the entire city comes from common parents: F. Scott Fitzgerald and Isadora Duncan."

> —*A visiting Hollywood writer.*

SAN FRANCISCO (1960)

OCT. 16. After 3½ days by train cross country, we (Gretchen and I) arrive in San Francisco, about which we had been told so much—all ecstatic—by our friends before departing. Even Khrushchev chose it as the one American city he would prefer to live in outside the Soviet Union. Was there really an American city about which one could become so rhapsodic? As seasoned New Yorkers ("I don't much care where in the world I am," once said George S. Kaufman, "as long as I can be at 58th St. and 6th Ave. every night at dusk") we are prepared for the "inevitable" letdown. It took no longer than to check into our hotel and repair to the nearest bar (two steps away), the

Bustles and Beaus, for San Francisco to reveal its unique charm. The Golden Gate city, having never quite gotten over its gaudy and roistering Barbary Coast days at the century's turn, this arch-typical café with its honky-tonk piano and voluptuous girls in tights sliding down from the dressing rooms on a brass pole, like firemen, was no lurid dead-fall, as these places can so often be, but a roguish prelude, indeed, to what was to become a fortnight's "afternoons of a faun," in and out of bars with their relentless *brio,* restaurants, parties, cocktail receptions, galas, picnics, *soirées* and films and films and films, for we are here for the 4th San Francisco International Film Festival.

The relevance of such details is more marked here than is usually the case with American cities. San Francisco lacks the hieratic disdain of New York, for instance; the latter's sharper contrasts give it an arrogant aloofness, as does its merciless stratification. But San Francisco does not take itself so seriously, it has the air of a city on a perpetual holiday and , indeed, it wears the motley of a merry-andrew among cities.

Dusk—far from the corner of 58th St. and 6th Avenue . . . the church bells outside our windows chiming, not "Adeste Fideles," but Wagner's "O Evening Star" as a prelude to the night. (On subsequent twilights we were to hear "April Showers," "I'll Be With You in Apple Blossom Time," etc., not a single religious hymn! Out in the street we encounter Union Square (as unlike our own as could be) at the crossroads of Geary and Powell St., the heart of the city, with its patrician St. Francis Hotel bordered by *fin de siècle* street lamps like in Paris and the low heavy-laden greenery, benches and daily band concerts, a bit of Monte Carlo transplanted. Newspaper kiosks, prettily designed and eye-catching, with their little signs (so unlike New York): "You are Welcome To Read Our Headlines"—and the flower stands, also like Paris, each trying to outdo the other in attractiveness. And the fiercely mustachio'd pirate in full regalia (complete with real pegleg) occupying his nightly stance at the Powell & Geary corner only too willing to tell whoever is curious as colorful a tale of his vivid past as his get-up promises. "Give my regards to Jack Dempsey!" he shouted after us. "He'll remember me!" Carillons pealing out odes to the night, flower-decked newsstands with the legend tacked over them, "A laugh, a tear, it's in the headlines here," pirates on street corners, the musical strains of

"My Fair Lady" coming through the palm trees of Union Square Park's nightly band concert (right around) . . . ! Is there any other place like it? After dinner we strolled the byways emanating from Union Square and came upon a short, narrow two-block deserted street, bordered by trees, lit by lamps amid the tree's foliage, and seemingly from the trees was wafted music, old Viennese waltzes, medleys of Victor Herbert and the like. It didn't matter that there was no one around to listen (except us, San Franciscans having, doubtless, long since taken this bit of *ars gratia artis* for granted) and we stood there enchanted. The street was Maiden Lane (again so unlike our own), wired not only for light but for music of the most dulcet kind. Never before did the speed of light or sound reach us so swiftly and surely than at this magical moment. We must have stood transfixed with wonder for some time for a passerby stopped and asked if we were lost. When we explained he smiled, "I know . . . I come over from Berkeley myself every week just to do what you're doing. I still can't get over it."

What a first day!

OCT. 17. We are off for a cruise of San Francisco Bay, via cable-car to Fishermen's Wharf. Those cable-cars on those heart-stopping grades! It's no place for someone with too vivid an imagination because if one of them ever didn't hold fast via its brake on the middle track which powers it, the chain reaction that would set in of the trolley (a veritable Toonerville Trolley, at that, with scores hanging on hazardously) hurtling down one steep hill after another right out into the bay, no doubt, would beggar description. But they hold, these relics, tho' it's better not to look back at the grade you're climbing (often as much as 65%) if you're queasy. Automobiles parked on these steep grades, drawn tight to the curb, give one the heebie-jeebies. Of course, riding in an automobile up these grades, with only the car's brakes and traction of the tires to hold you to the asphalt, especially when you stop for a red light just short of the summit of the road, is enough to shorten your life even if you do manage to climb over the top after what seems an eternity poised precariously between the vagaries of science and your Maker. For San Francisco is a city built on hills which gives one an ever new and startling vista of the town at almost every turning. And all around is the bay, that magnificent bay with its natural harbor spanned by the fabulous twin bridges, the Golden Gate and Bay Bridge. San

Francisco Bay—gateway to the Orient across the blue Pacific. We spend two hours on a sight-seeing cruise on it, after examining the exotic wares at Fishermen's Wharf, chiefly seashells, coral, etc. from the seven seas, and the profusion of fresh sea food—such lobsters and shrimp as you never saw! We also visit the old frigate, the Balclutha, built in Scotland for the American clipper trade, in the days of "wooden ships and iron men," and now a well kept and extremely informative nautical museum. Our most charming memory of the bay cruise—the little village of Sausalito, with its pink and white stucco houses perched precariously on the side of the hill rising from the bay, now an artists' colony with a view that could turn a horse into a poet (no offense meant, you lucky Sausalitans!). It is like a bit of the Mediterranean sea-coast along the Côte d'Azur.

Paris, Monte Carlo, the Côte d'Azur—we seem to be forever comparing the San Francisco area with some of the loveliest spots on earth, for truly it combines the best features of American and European cities. San Francisco is also the cleanest city I have ever seen. This fastidiousness is carried to even such an extent that the supervisor of maids in our hotel insisted on changing a bath mat because the color did not harmonize with that of the shower curtain. Tho' its population is less than a million, it is a bustling (but happily not overcrowded) metropolis with all that it means—luxury shops and hotels and every conceivable kind of eating place. Even its storied Chinatown, the largest in the world, is gaily festooned with illuminated lanterns and we spent the eve of the film festival dining and sight-seeing there. New York's twisting, winding, rather shabby Chinatown is, perhaps, more genuinely Chinese (in the D.W. Griffith sense) than San Francisco's but the Chinese colony of San Francisco is much larger and spills out in many "Chinatowns' via the many arteries of Grant St., which is the Bund, the Ginza, the Times Square of San Francisco's Chinese quarter. There is also a Japanese quarter.

For two days we have indulged ourselves in that witchery that only a tourist discovering a new and fabled city on his own can know—coming upon all its wonders gradually and, sometimes, even suddenly, with every turning. . . . Tomorrow night the film festival gets under way with a symposium heralding the inauguration of the biggest cultural and social event of the Autumn season. So to our beds with the "sugar plums" of this fascinating city dancing in our heads . . .

OCT. 18. We check into the Sheraton Palace, festival head-quarters. The Soviet delegation, just arrived by air from Moscow, host a caviar-vodka reception for the press. It consists of Alexander Karaganov, film and art critic (on the staff of Isskutsvo Kino), one of the festival's three judges (the other two being Darius Milhaud and myself), Grigori Chukhrai, director of *Ballad of a Soldier,* the Soviet entry, and the film's two stars, Zhanna Prokhorenko and Volodya Ivashov. Altho' Karaganov is the only one who speaks English, an official interpreter, Jerry Severn, has been assigned to them, as well as a lady "overseer" from the State Dep't. Karaganov thinks our films are, for the most part, too frivolous, tending to be "escapist" in their aims. Chukhrai feels that the director plays a far more decisive role in the Soviet Union than he does currently in Hollywood in determining the final shape of the film.

Tonight the World Affairs Council of Northern California will present, at the Metro Theatre where the festival films will be screened, a symposium, "The Role of Films in International Cultural Relations." The participants are Chukhrai, Jean Renoir and Edward Dmytryk, representing three markedly different worlds of film making. As it turned out, they spoke not on the scheduled subject at all but on the individual approach to film-making in the U.S.S.R., France and the United States. Chukhrai said that the box office did not determine what films were made in the Soviet Union and that once a project had been approved for production the director had complete autonomy. Edward Dmytryk confessed that Hollywood was guided solely by the box office but said that this did not always necessarily rule out good films. Renoir, the most voluble of the trio, was his usual effervescent and sardonic self. "In France," he said, "we are somewhere between the two." Although he had no illusions about film-making in France, which was rife with chicanery, the director does direct his picture, not the producer, or financial backers, and that even then the director is not always, necessarily, the true author of a picture; often the writer, when he is a good writer, is. He cited Jacques Prevert's work on *Les Enfants du Paradis* as an example. He, personally, tries to please his audience but does not follow their likes or dislikes in choosing his subjects. He got the biggest hand.

Renoir was originally to have been one of the judges but couldn't stay beyond a few days as he had to return to Beverly

Hills to finish the biography of his father for his publisher's deadline.

OCT. 19. Tonight the festival proper starts. Months of the most arduous work on the part of Irving Levin, festival founder and director, come to a climax. As the festival unwinds he will assume a role something like holding the reins of both chariots in *Ben Hur* single-handed in keeping the many strands of a major international cinema jamboree from flying off into as many dead-end directions. The gala opening feature is from France, *The Love Game,* a comedy from the "new wave," to "kick-off" on a gay note. It is preceded by a reception given by the French consulate. A capacity first night audience at the Metro Theatre applauds Mary Pickford, introduced by Mr. Levin as the "Queen of the Festival," following which we see the first films, three shorts, a witty cartoon from Rumania, *Homo Sapiens,* and two American satires, on modern art, *Day of the Painter,* and on the rah-rah aspects of American college life, *Pow Wow.* (All three will win awards — an auspicious start.) Alas, the feature, *The Love Game,* in the words of Anatole France, "confuses motion with pleasure." But nothing can dampen the gala mood of the occasion and there is a champagne party afterwards at the California Palace of the Legion of Honor.

OCT. 20. The day begins with a wine-tasting and chicken barbecue at Louis Martini's vineyards in Sonoma, Napa Valley, in honor of the Soviet delegation. A chartered bus carries an invited group to the picnic and the Russians are in a high mood; Zhanna Prokhorenko and Volodya Ivashov, 19 and 20 respectively, outfitted as an American cowgirl and cowboy, singing sad Russian songs and gay American rock and roll to the accompaniment of Volodya's balalaika. Romano Tozzi is along as is Maryan Talbot of the Vancouver Film Festival, among other journalists and special guests. On the way back, I ask Karaganov for "Red Moscow" and he obliges, at the top of his voice. Chukhrai is all smiles. Gretchen offers a medley of Russian and Spanish folk songs in which the others join in. Someone strikes up "Gaudeamus Igitur" which, surprisingly, is joined in by everyone in Latin. Truly we are well met here on this bus rolling along back to San Francisco for tonight's film, *Notti di Roma,* by Rossellini, a last-minute substitute for *La Dolce Vita,* withdrawn suddenly from the festival by producer Amato. (Rumors fly thick and fast. Why? At Cannes, *La Dolce*

Vita almost lost out to *Ballad of a Soldier*. Again it was competing against it, and with a Soviet judge on the 3-man jury. A case of discretion is the better part of valor? Perhaps.) *Notti di Roma* is about a girl masquerading as a nun who shelters three Allied soldier-escapees from a German prison camp. Eventually, all three, as well as her fiancé, are killed or rejoin their own forces. She is left alone on the night that Rome is liberated. All that she has left are her tears. A touching performance by Giovanna Ralli as the girl that will win an award.

The screening is followed by a champagne party given by the Italian consulate.

OCT. 21 Herbert Luft is up from Beverly Hills, as are Michael Lally and Paul Bartel, a "contingent" from 20th Century Fox—the latter's *Camel Rock*, a brief cartoon, being one of the most amusing entries *(hors concours)* in the festival. Tonight's picture is Denmark's *A Stranger Knocks*, about a widow who shelters a stranger overnight in her house, becomes his mistress and discovers he is the quisling who, during the Nazi occupation of Denmark, tortured her husband to death. The audience was shocked by two scenes more brazen in their salacity than anything ever witnessed on a screen in a non *sub-rosa* film. Who would ever have thought it from little Denmark? An English short, *The Visit*, was a bitter insight into lower middle-class life.

OCT. 22. Tonight's *Ballad of a Soldier* melts everyone to tears. A 19-year-old soldier gets a 6-day pass to visit his mother but encounters so many adventures on the way back to his village that he has time only for a hug and goodbye and must return to his outfit. He never returns. The war exacts him, too, as part of its toll. The awful waste of war is the moral. Perhaps it is sentimental—but go tell that to a mother who has lost her son in war. Afterward, festival director Levin gave a supper party at his home for the film's director and stars, who are jubilant at the unanimous reaction to their very moving film.

OCT. 23. Sunday—a double header, *The Enchanting Shadow* from Hong Kong by Run Run Shaw (here with his wife and attractive daughter) and *Macario* from Mexico, from a script by the mysterious B. Traven (author of *The Treasure of Sierra Madre*). The former is typical of the ghost stories beloved by the Chinese and the latter is an allegory stemming from a very old parable. Ignacio Lopez Tarso will win an award in the latter as the Mexican peon who always wanted to know what it was like to eat a meal that wouldn't be shared with his hungry family, which invariably left little for himself. Getting down to such basics, the film touched everyone. (Every program has its complement of shorts. *Deracinaments*, from France, dealing with psychotic drawings, will also win an award, as will *Roughnecks*, a documentary on oil-drilling from Canada.)

OCT. 24. Tonight's entry is the first of the two American films in competition: *Flight* by Barnaby Conrad from a John Steinbeck story (both are here) about a Mexican boy who kills a man in a café brawl, takes to the hills, is hunted down and shot. Everyone's intentions were of the best but something went wrong somewhere. Better was a Soviet short, *Revenge*, from a Chekhov story, about a jealous husband whose attempt at revenge on his wife's lover backfires.

Barnaby Conrad—one of the two balladeers *in excelsis* of San Francisco—the other being Herbert Caen, both chroniclers *sans pareil* of that dream city — Conrad, the debonair author of that unabashed valentine, *San Francisco: A Profile with Pictures* (perhaps the loveliest ode to a city anybody ever did), and Caen, journalist-Pepys, whose *San Francisco: City on Golden Hills*, embellished by Dong Kingman, by recalling the city's memorable folklore and legends of high doings, brings him to defend his nostalgia with "A healthy regard for tradition is not a weakness—'Memory,' said Thomas de Quincey, 'is the book of judgment.' " (I wish the audience could have seen Frank Stauffacher's little film, *Notes on the Port of St. Francis*, too, the sheerest poetry put to the service of a rhapsody on the city, and its companion film, *Sausalito*—both incomparable in American cinema annals.)

OCT. 25. Tonight is a double feature, Japan's *Diary of Sueko* and Poland's *See You Tomorrow*, preceded by a wry cartoon from England, *The Insolent Matador*. The Japanese film, based on the actual diary of a ten-year old girl, traces the misfortunes of a family, victim of the coal mining depression of 1953-54. Little Akiko Maeda will be included in a triple award to the role played by child-actors in the festival films, and Tanie Kitabayshi will win an award as the best supporting actress in the same film, as a meddling grandmother. The Polish film is a film about youth and like a fresh breeze but I seem to be the only one who finds this quality in it. I still stand by it.

OCT. 26. Tonight's picture is Germany's *A Man Goes Through a Wall* with Heinz Ruehmann repeating his stock ingratiating performance in the title role. I've been seeing Ruehmann at this sort of thing since the early thirties (since *Drei Tage Mittelarrest, u.s.w.*) and, with the exception of a valiant try as *The Captain of Koepenick,* he never did much else (except the police inspector in *It Happened in Broad Daylight,* which you can have, if you like Swiss *fondue.*) Afterwards, the Foreign Film Theatre Owners of Northern California threw a party in the foyer of the Fox Theatre, complete with music, dancing, balloons released at midnight, and general wassail. Maryan Talbot, all peaches and cream and heady effervescence, takes me on a tour of this brobignagian movie temple of the cinema's "golden age," today a gaudy "white elephant." It is here that I am "stopped in my tracks" by a lithesome lass, Corinna Lothar, attached to Irving Levin's festival staff . . .

OCT. 27. Tonight is another double bill, Yugoslavia's *Black Pearls* and Hungary's *Be Good All Your LIfe,* the former a sort of Slavic *Boys' Town,* predictable throughout, and the latter a sentimental Hungarian pasty. Both deal with the theme of justice gone awry. Laci Toth, the youngster in the Hungarian film, will be included among the triple honorable mentions for the best child performances. (Even when some of the festival films are not particularly distinctive, it is good to be reminded by them that people are pretty much the same the world over. There's your role of the cinema in international cultural relations, even if it seems to have very little effect politically as "ambassador of good will" etc. on the world's lawmakers.) But an American short (cartoon), *The Interview,* is a very funny commentary on the beat set.

OCT. 28. Hungary's *Immortality,* a short dedicated to the work of Gyorgy Goldman, a Jewish sculptor killed in World War II is a highly passionate film, that will also win an award. It introduces the feature of the evening, *Mein Kampf,* a Swedish documentary compiled from captured Nazi newsreels on the rise and fall of Hitler. The biggest crowd of the festival thus far has turned out to see it, with many turned away. From the sickeningly sweet smile of Hitler (like the hypocritical sweetness of ether before you lose consciousness) to the searing atrocities at the end and the awesome rubble of the "thousand-year Reich," the film drives home relentlessly its picture of the face of fascism as a salutary warning to mankind. It, too, will win an award, a special one created for it tho' with reservations

The author and Corinna at the grand old Fox Theatre in San Francisco dur-
ing the film festival there that year (1960) (Photo: Richard Brooks)

by Karaganov for the several hundred feet (perhaps even as much as eight minutes, he said) of excised footage showing the role of the Red Army in breaking the back of the Nazi Army in Russia. (A more complete version, with all this footage, was shown at Cannes, he said.) A Yugoslav cartoon, *Concerto for Submachine Gun,* took an award as a devastating satire on capitalism.

The Soviet delegation threw their own party afterwards around a long table laden with Russian delicacies and vodka, presided over by pretty girls in Russian costumes. Diane Varsi was there. The dancing was to strictly American jazz, however, despite the caviar and *blinis.*

(Here I might mention that Gretchen and I frequently were assigned the official Soviet car, a snappy white Cadillac flying the Soviet and American flags on its hood and whenever we drew up before the theatre for a screening we tried to look as Russian as we could, being the cynosure, along with our Soviet colleagues, of all eyes on the sidewalk from the ubiquitous mob invariably gathered there.)

OCT. 29. Another double-feature tonight: Czechoslovakia's *Romeo, Juliet and Darkness* and Israel's *They Were Ten.* The former retells the familiar Romeo and Juliet story against a background of the Nazi occupation of Prague. A Czech youth shelters a Jewish girl from the murderous fury of the Nazis when Heydrich is assasinated and both pay with their lives. It is far better than *The Diary of Anne Frank* and will win an award for the most original screenplay. Israel's *They Were Ten,* about the first refugee pioneers in Palestine before it became the independent state of Israel (in the 1890s) is simple, direct and affecting, tho' it will surely not attract a twentieth of the attention that *Exodus* will.

OCT. 30. A triple-header today with two in the afternoon, Pakistan's *My Country* and Korea's *Unheeded Cries,* and the second American entry, John Cassavetes' much-touted *Shadows* (the second version). The first can be written off as primitive stuff for native consumption, like most Hindu films, while the second, obviously influenced by American juvenile delinquency films, has a strong documentary interest which is better than all its contrived melodramatics. Little Sung Kian will complete the triumvirate of honorable mentions to the child actors who acquitted themselves so well at the festival.

The party at the Pakistan consulate is a welcome respite

afterwards. (Looking over these notes for the last week I see I have omitted to mention the late supper at Vanessi's for Jean Renoir and the "hard core" of the festival guests, including always the ubiquitous Russians; the *diner à quatre* to which the Milhauds invited Gretchen and myself at the Japanese "country-restaurant" adjoining the Metro Theatre; the two parties at the Iranian consulate, the second to celebrate the birth of an heir to the ancient Iranian throne; the outing to the Muir Woods to see the giant redwoods where the forest they form becomes a naturally vaulted gothic cathedral, this followed by a reception at the Coopers (he is a leading San Francisco exhibitor)*; and a motor trip to the Pacific, coming back through Golden Gate Park with its charming Japanese gardens and museum, harboring a small treasure of paintings one has seen only in reproduction. This may be also the place to mention my talk to a group of teachers from Sacramento State College, up for the festival, newspaper, radio and television interviews, including several radio interviews for the Pacifica Foundation and Canadian Broadcasting Company.

Preceded by four shorts including a withering commentary on horse-racing bettors from Poland (what surprising things have turned up at this festival!), came *Shadows* as tonight's entry from the United States. Some of the stars are here, too, Rupert Crosse, Tom Allen . . . Sloppily dressed, badly mannered and *gauche* in every way, they did neither themselves nor their film any good by their presence — nor could the film save them. If "an improvisation," as Cassavetes calls his film, perforce excuses a complete lack of form and banality of content (because that's life, man, that's life — life don't have no form, man, and you gotta be con*tent* with your *cont*ent, dig me, man?) then one must forget all the accepted canons of art and the disciplines of art. In Europe this film is accepted as "hot stuff" from the avant-garde of the American "new wave" and has gone over big in France and England, I understand. It may even find its audience here, too, among the rebels with and without causes. (I saw another "beat" film in Los Angeles a week or so later, *The Flower Thief,* so "improvisational" as to make *Shadows* look like a Jerry Wald picture by comparison.) Eisenstein also once made a revolutionary film, just as

---

*At the Coopers we met Evelyn Munchhausen, a direct descendant of the famous 18th century Baron Munchhausen and tale-teller extraordinary. Where else but in San Francisco would you find *her*?

rebellious for its time as *Shadows* is supposed to be, it was call-
ed *Potemkin* and it has the purity of form and classic discipline
of a Greek vase. Don't give me none of that "improvisation"
stuff, man. Mr. Cassavetes' next film, I hear, will be for Para-
mount. Will we again see the same economic leash tame the
same lion as tamed Stanley Kubrick (whose pre-*Spartacus*
work was, at least, disciplined)?

OCT. 31. A half-dozen assorted shorts preceded tonight's
entry from Holland, *Symphony of the Tropics*, a color
documentary of Surinam (Dutch Guiana). Very pictureseque
and interesting (I'm a pushover for all travel films). An after-
theatre block-party in front of the Metro followed the showing,
with Dutch music, beer and cheese.

NOV. 1. Tonight's the windup with Spain's *Little Guide of
Tormes*, adapted from a 16th century Spanish classic, one of
the earliest and best picaresque novels, which dealt with
"picaros" or rascals who had to live by their wits in a Spain
undergoing disastrous economic crisis. The original is full of
audacious truth and directness, revealing the various social
strata of the time. The film dilutes it all and makes its young
hero, Lazar, "cute" instead of desperate; its roguery of the
world humorous instead of bitter; its reaction against the ar-
tificial world of the then popular chivalric romances facetious
instead of meaningful. In short, this famous anonymous work
which presaged both *Don Quixote* and *Candide,* is treated
here as if it were a series of jumping off points for movie gags.
The backgrounds were lovely, tho'. Another Rumanian car-
toon by the creator of *Homo Sapiens,* called *The 7 Arts,* about
primitive man's discovery of the arts, was far wittier.

The festival is over!

That night, at a formal supper ball in the Sheraton Palace's
Garden Court, the festival awards are announced. *Ballad of a
Soldier* wins the Grand Prize. (Jerry Severn, who's been "miss-
ing" the last few days, turns up with a beautiful Eurasian gal he
met while conducting the Soviet delegation through China-
town. He has a parting gift for Gretchen, a handsome Kirghiz
hat.) Irving Levin receives Italy's Star of Solidarity from the
Italian consul. I receive an embrace from Grisha Chukhrai,
director of *Ballad of a Soldier,* and an invitation to come to
Moscow for the film festival there in 1961. We say "au revoir"
to the Milhauds, the gracious, witty Milhauds, to the genial
Lufts who invite us to dinner in Beverly Hills next week, to

Awards Ball that closed the 4th International Film Festival in San Francisco. On the dias, L. to R.: Mrs. Harold Zellerbach, Alexander Karaganov, U.S.S.R. jury member, the author, U.S. jury member, Madeline Milhaud, wife of Darius Milhaud, France, Darius Milhaud, jury member. Standing: Harold Zellerbach, festival sponsor, Irving Levin, festival host and director, Violet Shaw, daughter of Run-Run Shaw, festival entrant. (Nov. 1960) (Collection of the author)

Karaganov, to the valiant festival staff . . . Corinna and I have a last waltz and I toast her with a last glass of champagne following which I smash it against one of the pillars, which, as far as I'm concerned, officially ends the festival.

* * *

For three days we "recuperated" from the festival and then went to Hollywood, where we visited the Paramount Studios to watch two then current productions at work, Danny Kaye's *On the Double* and Truman Capote's *Breakfast at Tiffany's*. We made a pilgrimage to the old Chaplin studio, visited Grauman's Chinese Theatre where all the stars' sidewalk imprints are, browsed through the wonderful collection of film books and periodicals at Larry Edmund's fabulous bookshop, saw the so-called "Walk of Fame" along the sidewalks of Hollywood Boulevard with such "memorable" Hollywood names enshrined as Woody Herman, Evelyn Rudie, Don DeFore, Joni Janes, etc. but not Chaplin, which made the whole thing ridiculous. We spent hours criss-crossing the vast expanse of Los Angeles by automobile, visited the charming year-'round food fair that is the Farmer's Market, dined at the Lufts' and Fritz Lang's and spent hours winding in and out of that amazingly luxurious colony of residences of the film stars, directors and others that is Beverly Hills. Two memorable evenings were spent looking at old films from a private collection and it was there that I saw again, after all these years, Chaplin's now legendary and still marvelous *A Woman of Paris,* and, what is more, the rarest of rare film incunabula, the out-takes on *A Woman of Paris,* showing, in scene after scene, how Chaplin worked.

A week in Hollywood and environs went by quickly and I was due back in New York to resume my film class at City College by Nov. 15th.

On my return, I learned from festival director Irving Levin that the festival had been the biggest and best from a financial standpoint of the four thus far held. I was glad to hear this because I knew it had decidedly been an artistic and social success. Plans are already afoot for the 5th annual San Francisco International Film Festival next November. Accredited by the International Federation of Film Festivals in Paris, the San Francisco event is now one of the world's major film festivals, on a par with Cannes, Venice, Berlin and Moscow. With or without the support of Hollywood it will continue to grow in importance, if its past record is any indication. By next Fall, the American independents should be out in full force with the true American "new wave" of which the present appearances are doubtless only the half-gods, the Davidic Messiahs, before the genuine advent.

(Towards the end of 1978 a wave of crime engulfed the city as grotesque as it was sudden. "San Francisco Comes to Grips With Murders" was the caption on a news story in the New York Times on Dec. 11th of that year. Under a byline by Roger Wilkins it began —

"How does a city resurrect itself when its heart has been shot out? Especially a city like San Francisco, whose residents adore it and exult in showing it to visitors, facet by facet, as if it were a precious stone?" . . .)

Have you ever watched a bird carry a twig in its beak on its way to a fork in the branch of a tree where it deposits it and then flies off to get another twig, brings it back and puts it down across the first twig—thus beginning the building of its nest? It's not easy to see but I have seen it. One of the most touching sights is to see the inside of a pigeon's nest—the spotted eggs that will be hatched some day by the female. I have also seen an even rarer sight—two pigeons love-making, if that's the phrase for it. It happened on my window sill one morning. The female inclined her head on one wing and kept resting it there, her eyes closed, as the male pecked at her with his bill. They must have carried on like that for several minutes. That's all there was to it, then they both flew away, but while it lasted it was one of the most touching sights in nature I'd ever seen. Another time I saw a dead pigeon on a sidewalk and watched as another pigeon fluttered down and after pecking at it as if to wake it up, settled down to sit by it, apparently to wait for it to get up. Whales have been known, when one of their number in a school of them is beached, to move into shore and "stand by," waiting for it to free itself and rejoin them. City life for pigeons is tough because they have to scrounge for food and they seem always to be hungry. So would you be if all you had to eat was dirt, and only a pigeon can peck at nothing at all in the street and think it's eating. Withal, it is a world where birds glory in the soar and swoop of free flight and where whales and dolphins frolic, when the fishermen let them, churning the seas as they roll, sport and dive . . . "Save the whales!" is the current rallying cry, but we don't save them, we and the others kill them, just like we all kill each other, unaware that the killers will themselves one day be dead and that for a long time . . .

The assassination of President Kennedy, which catapulted the Sixties into becoming "the chamber of horrors" Alan Jay Lerner called it in his autobiography, "The Street Where I Live," showed that not only were we adept at killing—we could celebrate it (I'm not so sure that's not the right word for it) in high style as witness the elaborate funeral we gave the President. We can't order ourselves to prevent killings but we sure can give the victim one hell of a funeral, no?

Film people?

Since that's what would be expected of me in a book like this, I suppose, and since they are (in some cases were) people, too, with all that it implies — and would be accepted as such by the reader, I hope — here are some I knew . . .

During the German occupation of Paris, just before World War II, von Stroheim was in New York, as were so many other show business people, and artists in all the fields, who fled the Nazi juggernaut. He was doing a play, the Boris Karloff role in *Arsenic and Old Lace* at the old Fulton Theatre (formerly the Helen Hayes Theatre), across from the Paramount Hotel where I lived, and I used to visit him there. Once, Denise Vernac, his companion who came over on a visitor's visa with him (she was a French citizen but he had his naturalization papers long since), she had to make an exit from the country and then re-enter for a renewal of her visitor's visa, or some technicality like that. Just a matter of crossing the border into Canada and coming back. Tom Curtiss was with us backstage that night and Tom and I were given instructions on how we were to handle this so that Denise could make a re-entry and get back in without anything going wrong in the process. At the moment when he heard his cue, Stroheim gave us a parting shot, "Be careful," he said. "You can only — — — — this up once!"

We were in the old Barberry Room one night (before they dolled it all up so it's all but unrecognizable now to its old hardy perennials) dawdling after dinner — Stroheim, Denise, Tom and I (we were a foursome in those days, 1939-40-41) and as the evening wore on we'd occasionally look around, and, seeing others there, we kept talking. Then Denise said in a low voice, after looking around, "Those people we thought were others like us *are* really us — we've been seeing our reflections in the wall mirrors. We're all alone here, and I think the waiters want to go home." We left quickly.

Nights at the Stork Club — Stroheim, Denise, Tom Curtiss and me — once Chaplin caught Stroheim's eye and they exchanged smiles — another time it was Lillian Hellman. In both instances — there was never any question — Stroheim made swift brief visits to both their tables.

Of course, the big bash was the party Tom gave at the Hotel Astor (which is now one of the stars in the night sky along with so many other memories of dear, departed people, places and things) — the idea being to bring Stroheim and Thomas Mann together in a glittering ambiance that included financial backers for a super-film if ever there was one — Mann's own *The Magic Mountain*. Gifford Cochrane, who had brought over *Maedchen in Uniform* from Germany for its American distribution here with John Krimsky, was to have backed the venture. The party was preceded by a screening in Pat Powers' projection room of his production of Stroheim's *The Wedding March* (Parts One and Two) to show potential backers the artistry of Stroheim as a director who could be trusted to bring *The Magic Mountain* to the screen — that symbolic and philosophic treatment of modern man's problems on the highest level. Touching upon almost all the ideas and issues of the Twentieth Century, from psychoanalysis to relativity, from Eastern dogmatism to Western liberalism, *The Magic Mountain* (Der Zauberberg) was universally recognized as one of the monoliths of the modern world's literature. When Stroheim remonstrated weeks before that he hadn't read the book, we gave him a copy and told him to cram it down quick so he'd have some idea of what it was about before the party. He told us the night before the party, after he had just finished reading it (or at least he claimed he did) that "How can you make a picture out of that? It's about a bunch of tubercular people in a sanitarium in the Swiss Alps, fer Chrissake!" We were too deep in it now to back out. The party, like one of Trimalchio's feasts, was "the works," but we didn't have to back out, Cochrane did it for us, and said he was thinking of backing a film about the Civil War, instead, which interested him more, as I remember it. Anyway, nothing happened except that a lot of celebrities met each other — Franz Werfel, Lion Feuchtwanger, Max Reinhardt, Erwin Piscator, Rudolph Kommer, Karen Michaelis, Ernest Boyd, Lilly Darvas, Muriel Draper, Howard Dietz, Al Lewin, Hans Eisler, Klaus, Golo and Erica Mann and Dr. and Frau Mann, too, of course, Ference Molnar, Hugo von Hofmannsthal's son, Clare Booth Luce, S.N. Behrman, etc. I remember one incident when Dr. Mann, holding a small thin cigar, was looking for his pocket lighter and I offered him a light. He thanked me and said, "Do you really think *The Magic Mountain* can be filmed?" "No," I said. To which he replied, "Neither do I." (A dozen times since then there have been announcements — once even by Alexander Korda — and no one ever dared it. It's like all the rumors about filming Proust's *Remembrance of Things Past*, even with a screenplay by Harold Pinter, done and ready for filming — and yet no one dares that one, either. And that one even had a backer — the Rothschilds via Nicole Stephane — was still "no dice." And for the same good reasons — it can't be done. Look at the extent to which they missed their filming of *Ulysses* though they did rather better with *Portrait of the Artist as a Young Man*. Joyce and Eisenstein had talked about doing it when they met at Sylvia Beach's bookshop, Shakespeare & Co., in Paris, but Eisenstein told Joyce he had too much respect for the book's language to attempt to find a filmic equivalent for it and so he desisted.)

O tempora, O mores! Minne, from a Colette story, "Minne ou l'Ingenue libertine," told of a newly wedded wife who, failing to find connubial bliss with her husband, dallies with a couple of gentlemen, one of whom, an old rip of sly and urbane airs, despite the possibility of an easy conquest, smilingly rejects her, saying he does it only because it wouldn't be fair to her husband, who is his friend, and that "he'll wear this gallant gesture in his lapel like a flower." (Daniele Delorme was the girl and Jean Tissier the man, and the year was 1950.)

In *L'Atlantide*, G.W. Pabst's poetic fantasy after the novel of Pierre Benoit, Count Bielowsky, raving over the beauty of the white queen, Antinea, who rules the domain in which Legionnaire officer, Saint-Avit, finds himself a captive beneath the Sahara, says she is as beautiful as a goddess. "A goddess?" repeats Saint-Avit, incredulously. "Why not?" answers the Count. "Are not all women in some way divine?" We are a long way from that today (the film dates from 1932), a long dismal way.

If I had to choose the most felicitous use of image and sound in all cinema to date I would choose Prokofiev's music for Eisenstein's victory celebration after the battle of Pskov in *Alexander Nevsky*. The images of musicians playing their pipes and rattling their tambours furiously intercut with one blasting a double pipe, which at the same time celebrates the wedding of the two couples, is one of the high enchantments of the screen. Both Eisenstein and Prokofiev in their abstractions of instruments and music wedded to each other to form a single exultant clamour of trills and rills achieved something absolutely unique in the sound-film and never matched for joyousness either before or since.

One of the strangest episodes I ever saw in a film—was it in Rossellini's 1958 documentary of India?—I forgot—showed a trained monkey on a street in Calcutta, dressed in a little gold-braided scarlet uniform taking his feathered *shako* off for coins while his master played an organ grinder, when suddenly the old fellow keeled over in collapse and died right there on the sidewalk. The crowd around the monkey dispersed (people collapsing on the sidewalk obviously being a common sight in Calcutta) and the monkey was left to fend for himself. He wanders off and we next see him (via a dissolve) approaching a clearing in a forest where there is a "Monkey House" where a *guru* sits whose incantations and bizarre medicinal rituals are supposed to heal the sick who come to him. He is surrounded by his own monkeys who, when they see the city monkey in his bright uniform approaching them, set up such a noisy chatter that they frighten the city monkey away. They don't want any part of this oddball. The last we see of him he is scurrying away from tree to tree in a panic . . .

I used to sit with Josef von Sternberg at the broker's, E. Hutton's in Radio City, watching the board (he was a heavy investor) for what seemed like hours without end, neither of us saying much. It reminded me of Paulette Goddard sitting alongside Diego Rivera as he was doing one of his murals in Mexico City, the two hardly exchanging a word for hours on end, too, until Paulette, wearying of the ordeal, would finally start to climb down, with Rivera looking sadly after her saying, "I see I'm beginning to bore you."

Speaking of Paulette Goddard reminds me that Erich Maria Remarque, whom she subsequently married, was once introduced to an American girl abroad some years before the last war. When she asked him why he had never visited America, he said he told her that he knew only a few English sentences. "What are they?" she asked. *"How do you do?"* he replied. *"I love you. Forgive me. Forget Me. Ham and eggs, please."* "With those," smiled the girl, "you could tour my country from Maine to California."

One of the things Sternberg did say to me during those long hours at Hutton's, strangely enough, was that one of his few (very few, as it happened) favorite directors was, of all people (considering their widely divergent styles), Luis Buñuel — the same Luis Buñuel who had said that the motivating forces of his art were the carnality and greed of the world. Another Sternberg named was Henri Clouzot, just as widely divergent. (Look deep into Sternberg's work and you will see that they were not *that* widely divergent.)

Fritz Lang told me that Erich Pommer, production chief at Ufa, the first big Berlin film studio in the good old days, used to warn his directors to restrain themselves from having affairs with their leading ladies while their films were still in production. "Hold off until the picture is finished," he'd say. "You want your audience to feel toward her the way you do, right? Then wait till the picture is in the can. After that, you can have all the affairs you want. It won't matter then. Am I clear?"

When Lang came to Hollywood, his mascot was Mickey Mouse, a figure of whom was mounted on Lang's travelling cameras and went wherever they went. Later, he was given as a birthday gift a large stuffed animal—a chimpanzee—who he claimed was addicted to martinis. "He's not a chimpanzee," he would say, "he's a gin-panzee." Lang told me that when he described to the 17-year-old Brigitte Helm, while interviewing her for the dual roles of the good and evil Marias for *Metropolis,* the seductive dance she'd have to do as the evil Maria, she reached for her coat and made for the door. "What kind of film are you making?" she protested. "Anyway, I didn't want to come here, it was my mother's idea. I never wanted to be an actress!" "What did you want to be?" asked Lang. *"Kinderarzt!"* (Children's doctor) "Come," he said, taking her hand, "sit down . . . " And he talked her into it. That was in 1925. She remained on the screen till 1936. She even visited Lang in Hollywood once.

In 1967 I was with Lang at the Montreal Film Festival, where he was one of the three guests of honour, the other two being John Ford and Jean Renoir. One day a cable came for Lang, inviting him to a symposium on German screen expressionism, at which he would be the principal speaker. It was signed by Lotte Eisner. On the day he was to fly to Berlin for the event, I accompanied him in a taxi to the airport. "Quick," he said, "tell me, what is 'expressionism'? What does Lotte mean by that?" "You're kidding," I replied. "You, the great Pooh-Bah of German screen expressionism, ask me a question like that — at a time like this? We'll be at the airport in a few minutes!" "Come on, quick!" he said. "I wouldn't kid about

Fritz Lang and the author in the American Pavillion at the 1967 Montreal Exposition. (The smiling damsel on the huge mural in the background is, of course, Marilyn Monroe.)

The author and Fritz Lang in the French Pavillion at the Montreal '67 Expo' . . .

a thing like this. Tell me—I have to say *something!*" So in the remaining few minutes I tried to give him a "crash course" in the art movement, expressionism, that heightened reality which I told him was rooted in the miasma of Verdun in 1915-16 out of which came that black flower of German screen expressionism, *The Cabinet of Dr. Caligari.* Well, and so forth. Lotte wrote me later that he delivered an eloquent speech on the subject.

The point of it all is that Lang, like others of the big directors — Chaplin and Stroheim come immediately to mind — didn't know the big words (certainly not like the intellectual Eisenstein did). They knew only one thing: how to make good films.

Lang told me once he found a girl in his hotel room one night as he came in. She rose to meet him — she was nude. He asked her how she got in and she said via an arrangement with the bell-hop. (It was the St. Moritz.) He asked her what she wanted and she smiled. "You know," he said, "there was a scene like this in a film I once saw, God help me, called *The Bachelor and the Bobby Soxer.* The girl was Shirley Temple, but fully clothed, and the man was Cary Grant. So you see how different it was from this!" He reached for her clothes flung over a chair and told her to dress. "You're too young for this," he said he told her, "and I'm too old." And he pressed a twenty-dollar bill into her hand. "Go, my child," he told her at the door, and he kissed her on the forehead. "May God bless you — so far He hasn't."

It probably wasn't generally known that Lang and George Antheil, composer of the notorious "Ballet Mécanique" and other compositions of our "steel, stone and glass age," but who also wrote some very effective movie music scores (especially for Ben Hecht), were close friends. Both had some of the same fetishes where women of certain propensities were concerned. (Let it go at that.) But one night at dinner, the conversation turned to music. "One of my frustrations," said Antheil, "and I have all categories of them, has been that I haven't had a chance to do something I've always wanted to do in my movie scores — to write satirical Oriental music. To kid Oriental music. Nobody knows about it — they keep talking about the "Ballet Mécanique", but I've never been assigned to do the score of a film where I could use that kind of music." I was in Carnegie Hall the night his "Ballet Mécanique" — scored for brass, mechanical pianos, sheets of galvanized tin and aeroplane propeller, as well as a set of electric bells — was given. When the propeller was turned on, those in its path turned up their jacket collars against the high wind and one man tied his handkerchief to the end of his cane and waved it, as a flag of truce, in token of the audience's surrender. It was Antheil who, when he gave a piano recital in Budapest once (he was a formidable pianist), reached into his hip pocket, after he sat down on the piano bench, and took out a revolver, which he placed on the instrument. This, he told journalists with a straight face after the concert, was to defend himself in case anyone tried to start something. That happened before, he said, and he wasn't taking any chances.

You know the story of the beggar into whose cup someone dropped a gold sovereign? Lubitsch told it to me once as one of his favorites because it illustrated one of his best discoveries — the dramatic virtue of irony, with which he imbued all his work. "Well," thought the beggar, "a gold sovereign! It's not every day that that happens!" He rushed to the bank to cash it into banknotes but after the cashier looked at it he gave it back to him and said it was a counterfeit. Outside, the beggar looked at it again. It shimmered in the sun, still, and he wondered what use he could make of it that would make his life better. Then he thought of the girl who worked the same block he did. He went up to her and let the coin glisten before her eyes. She smiled and nodded. He followed her home and they spent the night together. The next morning, when he reached into his pocket to pay her, the coin wasn't there — there was a hole in his pocket instead. In abject tones he tried to tell her of his misfortune . . . that he'd lost the coin . . . he was terribly sorry and all that . . . but she was furious and began throwing things at him. While ducking the flying crockery, he managed to tell her, "Calm down, calm down . . . it was only a counterfeit, anyway!"

That," Lubitsch went on, "was a capitalist joke. But the Communists had their irony, too. In a Bucharest classroom, students were being taught the virtues of Communism — solidarity, one for all and all for one, etc. "Who will give me an example of true Communism?" asked the teacher. Up came Popescu's hand. "I helped a little old lady cross the street," he said. "Fine!" said the teacher. "Who else?" Whereupon Monescu raised his hand. "I helped Popescu help the little old lady across the street," he said. "Great!" said the teacher. "That's

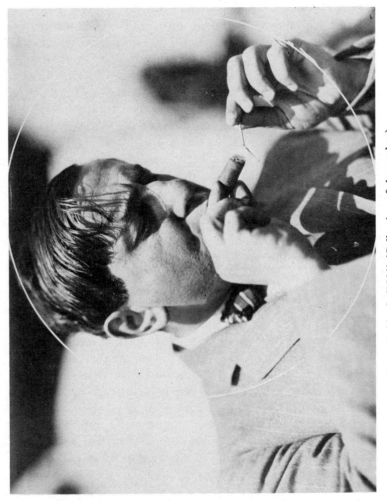

Ernst Lubitsch (1930) (Collection of the author)

the true Communist spirit! One more?" To which Dinicu raised his hand. "I helped Popescu and Monescu help the little old lady cross the street," he said. "Marvelous!" said the teacher, her eyes shining. "But, tell me," she added, "Why did it take three husky boys like you to help one little old lady cross the street?" "Because," said Popescu, "she didn't want to cross."

"But you know what the beginning of the idea of irony was for me?" said Lubitsch. "In Berlin, 1918, right after the war, right after Germany's terrible defeat, during all that misery. A story typical of the times made the rounds, about a man so bereft of everything that he decided to end a life no longer worth living. So he bought himself a rope to hang himself but the rope, like everything else in those days, was *ersatz* (synthetic), and it broke. Taking this as a sign from Heaven that he should live, he went to a café for a cup of coffee but that, too, was *ersatz*, it made him ill and he died."

"That," he said, "was the beginning for me of what became known as the Lubitsch touch."

Lubitsch once told me that two of his favorite "Lubitsch touches" weren't by him at all — one being the placard in the cloakroom of the pre-World War I Budapest club reading, "Members may not bring their mistresses as guests unless they are the wives of other members" — and the other being Melchiors Lengyel's (he did the original stories for Lubitsch's *Ninotchka* and *To Be or Not To Be*) "Kissing a woman's hand is never the right thing to do; it is either too much or too little."

Robert Flaherty, father of the documentary film, whose *Nanook* and *Moana* are, perhaps, the two most sacred icons of all such, once said to me, "When people ask me what my favorite film is I always tell them what they expect me to say, namely, Dovzhenko's *Earth* — why should I upset them with anything else? It's a great film and all that. But between me and you," and here he giggled, "my favorite film is Lubitsch's little sex comedy, *Kiss Me Again*." In all the years since it came out, 1925, I never met anyone else who ever saw it besides me and Flaherty. (I've written it up in my book, *The Lubitsch Touch*.) Come to think of it, one other whom I met saw it — Richard Watts. No one else.

In Harry d'Arrast's film, *A Gentleman of Paris*, Adolphe Menjou uncrosses his fiancée's crossed legs, takes the cigarette from her mouth, and pulls her skirt down. He wants her to be a proper young lady. Forty-six years ago we thought this was sweet and despite our being engulfed with waves of the current pornography, it's still sweet, and was even in the films of Lubitsch which gave vent to his cockahoop sense of play (not only him but Preston Sturges, too). In the films of Lubitsch, women always were treated as ladies. Good manners stood duty as morals. But beneath all the romping and hilarity there was a biting criticism of social and moral corruption (*vide Three Women* and *Trouble in Paradise* especially) . . . It was humor after the manner of Molière, in which the froth covered a bitter ale.

"Lubitsch, who was my mentor," said Joseph Mankiewicz, director of two films that Lubitsch would have been proud to sign, *A Letter to Three Wives* and *All About Eve*, "could show more honest-to-God sexuality by having a girl go up to a door and open it or not open it than any of the wide-screen genitalia. Copulation has become what we used to call action. It's replaced mixing the martini or lighting the cigarette. That's why I'm not writing now. I don't think audiences listen to the screen anymore. They come to stare."

The thing about Lubitsch was that dexterity with sex themes that enabled him to out-fox the censors of the time and which tickled even such literary aristocrats as Edmund Wilson, who couldn't abide movies (tho' he especially doted on Lubitsch's *Kiss Me Again, Three Women* and *Lady Windermere's Fan*). I have reproduced a scene from *Three Women* which featured Marie Prevost as one of them, so subtly slinky that the censors couldn't touch it though she was the veritable incarnation of the cloven sex in it, a walk-up bacchante, exuding a fragrance of *fraises des bois* in clotted cream. (In my book, *The Lubitsch Touch.*)

Withal, Lubitsch made of his audiences connoisseurs, not a letter sent me by Gene Stavis, then director of the Cinématheque at the Metropolitan Museum of Art, where I delivered an address on the closing night of their Lubitsch retrospective, which they called "The Lubitsch Touch."

The Metropolitan Museum of Art

Fifth Avenue at 82nd Street, New York, N.Y. 10028   212-TR 9-5500

May 31, 1978

Mr. Herman G. Weinberg
228 West 71st Street
New York, N.Y.

Dear Herman,

   I couldn't let this opportunity pass without
telling you how much we at the Cinematheque ap-
preciated your introduction to TROUBLE IN PARA-
DISE on the closing night of "The Lubitsch Touch".
There is no-one on earth who could have better
prepared an audience for that experience and I
consider us lucky indeed to have you so much
with us and so close by.

   As long as the Cafe Ernst has such a capable
and knowledgeable maitre d', there is little to
fear from the fast-food operations of today.

                              Prosit!

                              Eugene Stavis
                              Cinematheque Director

VANCOUVER (1961)

The British Empire is no longer what it used to be and that's not news except that I found an outpost, one of its few remaining outposts, if that's what we may call it, in Vancouver, British Columbia, Canada, hard by the Pacific, engulfed by a beautiful harbor. And that was where one of the earliest of the Vancouver Film Festivals took place, and to which Gretchen and I were invited (I to serve on the festival jury).

Just as the Thirties, which began with the desolate depression years following the stock market crash of 1929, marked the blithe Little Theatre years for me in Baltimore, the Sixties, however meretriciously they began politically, socially and artistically, marked what were to become our "festival years," for Gretchen and me—San Francisco, Vancouver, Montreal, and then New York.

Norman McLaren, high priest of the animated film, working out of the National Film Board of Canada in Montreal, Kashiko Kawakita, ambassadress-at-large to the world's film festivals representing Japan, and I were the judges at the Vancouver International Film Festival that year.

But first I must tell you we had competition during the whole fortnight of the festival screenings—none other than the stripper, Lili St. Cyr, who, if not the Heifetz (that was the incomparable Hinda Wassau, remember?) of the burlesque theatres, was certainly their Fritz Kreisler (begging both their pardons, Heifetz and Kreisler, *bien endendu!*), *schwarmerei*, *schlagober* and all. And who of us could compete with her? We didn't try—we just pretended she wasn't there and went on about our business.

Our business, apart from viewing the films, was largely social — teas, cocktails, dinners, and when the governor-general of the province was in attendance, we toasted the Queen — "To Her Majesty, God bless her!"

We were interviewed by the local press, of course, and McLaren exuded the charm and whimsy for which he was famous—being in person just like his charming and whimsical little films. Madame Kawakita hoped, she said, that international film festivals like this one would help cement good-will between nations, since so many of them were now having film festivals, all for the same purpose—to foster international good-will (apart from business). "But," said I in one of my interviews, as I recall, "don't look to the movies to save the world.

Norman McLaren (1963) (Photo: National Film Board of Canada)

Surely, there must be surer ways, too."

Well, and then Victoria, on the way back by boat to Seattle, another outpost of the old Empire, with that old *grande dame* hotel named after the Queen, and, by the looks of her, very fittingly, too. Then Seattle and home.

Moon over Montreal . . .

In a little black Volkswagen driven by Norman McLaren through the evening drizzle to the Isle St. Hélène for the party after the gala opening at the Loew's Theatre of François Reichenbach's *Un Coeur Gros Comme Ça*, a *film gros comme ça*, which inaugurates the third annual film festival here.

Also in the car are Guy Glover and Gretchen. I tell Norman of John Grierson's recent lecture at the Museum of Modern Art, after which, during the question and answer period from the audience, I was tempted to ask, "What are The 39 Steps?" but resisted it. Gretchen tells Norman of Grierson's discussing the composing by Auden of the memorable narration for *Night Train*. "This is the night train," she began, "crossing the border . . . " And Norman picks it up as we turn to cross the Jacques Cartier bridge over the St. Lawrence . . .

> *Bringing the cheque and the postal*
> > *order,*
> *Letters for the rich, letters for*
> > *the poor,*
> *The shop at the corner and the girl*
> > *next door . . .*

We are on the little island in the middle of the river and Norman rolls down the car's window so we can smell the wet grass.

The St. Hélène Restaurant, where the festival celebration takes place each year, used to be a gunpowder magazine. Nevertheless, we raise our glasses of Montrachet and I offer a toast, the one Lea proposed in Morand's *Open All Night:*

> *To our health which is so dear to us,*
> *And which is so necessary to us,*
> *Because with health we can earn money,*
> *And with money we can buy sugar,*
> *And with sugar we can catch flies!*

The contingent from New York includes the Schlossers from the Carnegie Hall Cinema, Rudi Franchi, Marshall Lewis, Michael Burton, Robert Breer, Arnold Eagle and Bill Starr of the AFFS. Louis Marcorelles, just over from Paris, asks me, "Do you know Jonas Mekas? Eugene Archer? Andrew Sarris?" It's his first trip to North America and he's glad, he says, to find it just as big as he thought it would be. The festival is officially launched by Canadian actor, director, and recent Vancouver festival juror, Claude Jutra, the Sarasate of the Twist, doing his "Sacre du Festival" dance with a dusky nymph (the star of his first feature).

The evening is the usual *succès fou:* the orchestra weaving garlands of music endlessly around the dancers, the Montrachet flowing from bottomless magnums, the guests crowding the gigantic buffet as at one of Trimalchio's feasts. Gretchen and I stand in awe before a magnificent, ravishingly garnished whole Nova Scotia fresh salmon, at least a yard long. This is the second year we've looked at one like this one here and next year we hope to get up enough *savoir faire* to command the waiter behind the buffet to cut off a slice. Later, in a corner, over their plates, the ciné-buff group of Marcorelles, McLaren, and I discuss the eighth art far into the night, broken only by intermittent excursions to the buffet for coffee. (Brandy and cigars are in plentiful supply.)

I am on a panel discussion taped at the National Film Board for a television film on the new experimental cinema which the CBC will show this Fall and which New York may also see. While there, McLaren showed us around the Film Board, including his own work room: a work-table with rewinds, colored inks and pens, and a frosted glass square in the center (which lights up) covered with multi-hued patterns of paper in all manner of shapes. All around were bins and racks of film lengths, and a large bulletin board covered with souvenirs of his world travels and drawings by his friends, including two of Gretchen's.

We meet Evelyn Lambert, Norman's genial assistant. The room is absolutely gay with its multitudinous colors and designs. "So this is where it all starts!" I exclaim . . . "Exactly the way I thought it would look." In the commissary afterwards we are joined by the two Guys — Glover and Coté — and interest runs high among the Canadians (Arthur Lipsett, of the incisive little anti-world madness film, *Very Nice, Very Nice,* comes over too) about the American "new wave," the Charles Theatre and the salutary work it is doing for new young filmmakers, and all the sudden filmmaking activity in New York — underground and above ground.

Montreal — a Russian's idea of what New York is like. Rudi Franchi describes it: "All those gigantic smoked meat places!" Indeed, every second place is a restaurant along the main boulevard, most announcing the merits of their smoked meats,

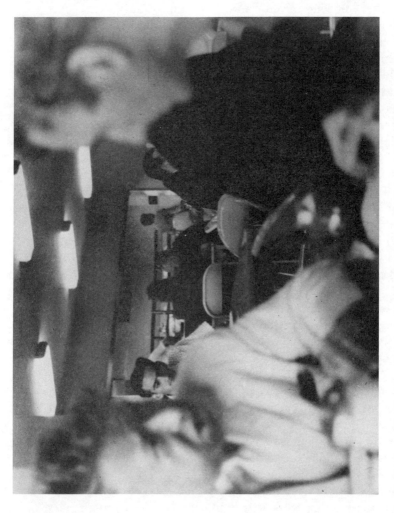

The author with Norman McLaren, National Film Board, Montreal (1962) (Photo by Gretchen)

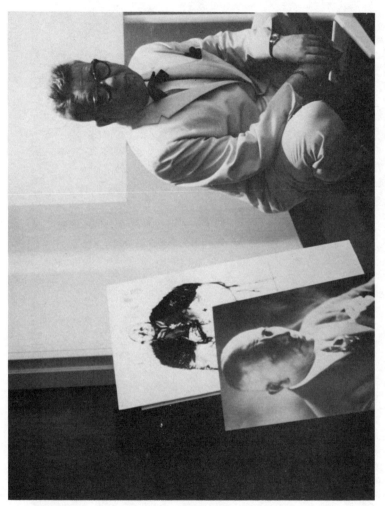

The author, mounting the Stroheim Exhibit at the Place des Arts, Montreal, (1962)

Gretchen (1961) (Photo by the author)

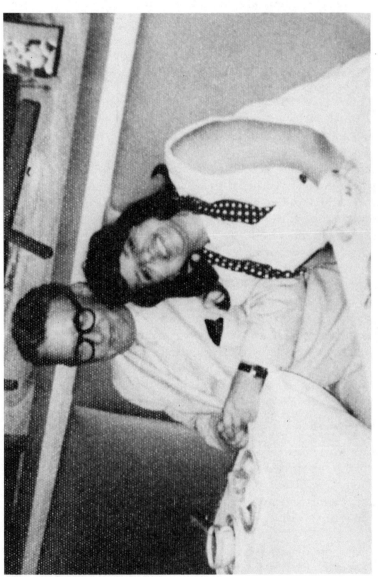

The author and Gretchen, during the Montreal Film Festival (1962) (Photo by Marc Sorkin)

the local specialty. Garish neon signs set St. Catherine Street ablaze at dusk while at night, dominating the scene, a large neon cross on Mount Royal shines high above the city.

A one-week festival's events come thick and fast: besides the thrice-daily showings of new films at the festival theatre, there were fringe screenings midnights at the Elysée for the New York group, including amusing shorts made by the French *nouvelle vague* bunch in their pre-feature days; the exposition of film posters from the world over at the Place Ville Marie, Montreal's stunning new skyscraper (right out of *Metropolis*), at which we awarded our own first prize to the Czech, Jiri Salamoun, for his superb drawing of Erich von Stroheim as Rauffenstein in *La Grande Illusion,* the nightly sessions, after the festival showings, at the Kino Club in the stately Hotel Windsor where the buffs gathered to eat and drink, dance and talk till two A.M.; the quasi-surrealist incident of three workmen entering the fifth floor hotel bedroom of Mrs. Schlosser when the lunchtime whistle blew and they found themselves right outside her window; the candle-lit tables at the Kino Club on the night when the lights suddenly went out at one A.M., a mystery that remained unsolved to the end; the showing of the complete *Earth* of Dovzhenko, preceded by Mme. Dovzhenko's touching greeting to the festival read by a spokesman; the Russian *Peace To Him Who Enters* with its lusty comment on militarism (of a baby inadvertently peeing on the rifles parked across a bed by the soldier-guests at a party) that brought spontaneous laughter and applause from the audience; Brazil's *O Pogador de Promessa* ("The Given Promise") which made them gasp; Dan Drasin's *Sunday,* a short on the folk-singing "riot" earlier that year in Washington Square, in New York City which left them in bewildered silence until a small New York group started applauding which "opened the dike" to the flood of applause that followed. Over all, Germain Cadieux and Pierre Juneaux, festival heads, hovered over merriment and mishap with equal aplomb, with cool, patrician equanimity.

But on the surface, at least, all is serene. Claude Jutra dances the festival out each night at the Kino Club, and it rains almost every day. But, *tant mieux,* as they say here, it will "soften the ground" for next year's festival!

COFFEE, BRANDY & CIGARS

I had a very popular column over the years called "Coffee, Brandy and Cigars" and I made one of them entirely of excerpts from letters I'd received from various friends in the arts. Written in 1963.

Edward Sackville-West once said you could tell more about a man from the letters he receives than the ones he writes. Leafing through the accumulation of years, I select these few fugitive pieces at random, excerpts presented in no particular order—sometimes informative or revelatory, sometimes whimsical or facetious, sometimes sentimental or nostalgic—all bound together by the garland of the arts.

A poem from novelist Joseph Freeman, "On Hearing Herman Weinberg in His Film Class," at which René Clair's *Sous les toits de Paris* was shown:

> *It's all true; we were there*
> *When Spring came on with rain on a Renoir street*
> *And Eros telegraphed on cobblestones*
> *With lovers' feet.*
> *Faces were innocent,*
> *Weapons small,*
> *Even the apache was magnanimous*
> *Before the Fall.*
> *The roaring smoke and glare of a passing train*
> *Obscured the inconclusive fight;*
> *No blood was shed that night.*
> *Death was not yet despot of the world;*
> *Right knew limits, so did wrong;*
> *And under all the roofs we heard,*
> *Above the self-delusion and the cant,*
> *The golden phoenix chant*
> *His ever-recurring song.*
> *Both rivals lost the girl*
> *To the faithful, astonished friend;*
> *This was the Happy End.*
> *The bombs drove underground to wait*
> *For the next turn of the wheel of fate*
> *When the Spring rains*
> *Will come again.*

A note from Ben Hecht commenting on an earlier installment of this column in which he reminisces wistfully about his own youthful walks through the garden of the arts: "It was the best time of all."

A "fan letter" commending me for my titles for *Sundays and Cybele* but adding fretfully, "Why do you insist on spelling 'all right' as one word?" Which reminds me of the late Sherwin Cody's frantic missives to me on the same subject. I hope that in Heaven, where he surely is, he finds both usages tolerantly accepted, else what is Heaven for?

ORSON WELLES

A letter from Orson Welles: "By long practice, I generally refrain from reading reviews of my own movies or plays. Through the years I've found an uncomfortable majority of my critics to be the opposite of encouraging, and I have a weakness in this matter: I tend to be very impressed by almost any reasoned attack on my work which may get into print. But I did read your review (in *Film Culture*). You kindly lulled my suspicions by sending it to me and, besides, there has been so very little written about *Mr. Arkadin* in English at all. The result was a very happy surprise. Unluckily for my professional ego, I have never been able to take a good review quite as seriously as a bad one but I must tell you that your generous appraisal was deeply appreciated. What really pleased me was not so much that you liked *Mr. Arkadin,* but that you liked it for what I take to be the right reasons. This, of course, is the ultimate compliment . . . "

From Symon Gould, a pioneer in the art cinema movement in the United States back in the Twenties, on the launching of *Potemkin* here:" . . . As I remember it, those present at the premiere of *Potemkin* in Gloria Swanson's penthouse at 58th and 6th Ave. were Mal St. Clair, Adolphe Menjou, John S. Cohen, Jr., Dick Watts, Lewis Milestone . . . "

TOM CURTISS AND VON STROHEIM

From Tom Curtiss, *Variety* correspondent and entertainment editor of the Paris Tribune: "How can I apologize for the long silence? . . . Whenever Denise, Erich (von Stroheim) and I are together we speak of you and, in the Kipling phrase, 'raise our glasses towards you' . . . The Tribune work goes on and widens. I now do theater, films and night-clubs, as my colleague, Art Buchwald, is concentrating on his N.Y. column . . . Von is working on the synch score of *The Wedding March* . . . I haven't seen it in years now. Is *The Honey-*

moon print still available? . . . I went to London last week to see some shows and Dick Watts, who is there for the opening of *The Moon Is Blue*. Diana Lynn, his (then) current girl friend, has the lead and has made the play into a hit. She's charming but I wish she was playing something else. Ward Morehouse gets to London tomorrow for a week and I may go back to see him and a few more plays. The London theatre is fine but London life is dreary after Paris . . . "

From Tony Richardson: "I've been meaning to write you ever since I got back (to London) but my life has been in even more chaos than usual. This has been largely because an uncompromising girl with a child and two lovers (for use and pleasure respectively) has been sitting in my flat. In the meantime I've had to sit on the doorsteps of all my friends. However, she's gone now."

From Karl Freund: "One of the interesting stories about Murnau's life was his friendship with Walter Spies, who lived on the island of Bali. Spies was an excellent painter and musician, handsome, the son of a very fine Baltic family. 'Civilization' at the end of the First World War proved too much for him, so he decided to run away from it and start a new life in the Dutch East Indies. Murnau, however, could never forget Spies, and many times attempted to persuade Ufa to make a South Seas picture so he could see Spies again. While he came quite close to fulfilling that desire during the filming of *Tabu* in Tahiti, I don't think Murnau actually ever did see Spies again. Spies, who was known to all travellers to Bali, including Noël Coward, Vicki Baum, Miguel Covarrubias, died as a prisoner when the boat on which he was being transported to a concentration camp was torpedoed during the Second World War."

'WICKEDEST EYES IN THE WORLD'

From Anielka Elter, the masked girl-musician in Prince Danilo's seduction scene of Stroheim's *The Merry Widow*, once publicized as "the girl with the wickedest eyes in the world": "What a shame that one gets to be old and the wicked eyes are not so wicked anymore. I was a Hollywood girl when the going was good and the most interesting or the craziest people were always interested in me. I was a musician in *The Merry Widow*, a girl with a mask, which Stroheim saw as a temptation of evil. I wore what in those days we used to call "A couple of flowers and nothing to pin them on.' As always in Stroheim films, I was also a face on the cutting-room floor. He shot a cigaret out of my mouth in that picture. I was insured at Lloyds for one day but the scene wasn't shown. I knew 'Von' very well, really well. Some of the parties, with lots and lots of drinking which he enjoyed enormously, were just terrific. Once he told how, in Austria, officers, after a night of spree, would hop out of the windows into the deep snow, their batmen holding up sheets for them. There were always some in the wild party scenes who, being well loaded, tried the same. There were broken legs, blood flowing — a wonderful mess.

"Once he decided my hair needed washing and broke a dozen eggs on my head and poured champagne on it as fast as he could. I could tell stories like this 'till the cows come home. But later he would not have it and did not like to speak about it. There was a wedding in Vienna's Stefansturm (St. Stephen's Cathedral), for instance, a real wedding of his camera-man, Hal Mohr — the church being one of the sets for *The Wedding March.* I was the bridesmaid, Stroheim the best man, but we all had so much 'developer' out of the glass basins where they developed the film that none stood straight during the ceremony. I was one of Elinor Glyn's pets and she was quite a type too . . . During the war I became some sort of a Mata Hari but someone slipped up, not me, and I went to prison. It was pretty tough. I was actually in front of a firing squad at one point. My prison experience left me physically ruined by dysentery and infections and my health is very precarious but since I've travelled a great deal and studied a bit I can now make a living as a writer . . . 'The wickedest eyes in the world' . . . good old Hollywood! 'She prays daily to a god of love.' What nonsense was perpetrated in the name of publici-ty. Old father De Mille wrote me saying, 'I shall never forget how beautiful you were and how brave.' Well, I was by no means ravishing, I think. But look at my generation today . . . Garbo . . . I remember the days when she was in love with Jack Gilbert; she looked as if she had a light shining from within. Don't think me sentimental. I'm quite down to earth now. It's only that old scrapbook . . . "

From S.T. Carrier: "I do not know whether or not my wife, Anielka Elter, answered your last letter. It is with very great regret that I have to tell you that she died two weeks ago."

Again from Tom Curtiss: " . . . I covered the Venice film

festival and saw a great deal of von Sternberg which was very pleasant. In fact I was booked to go to Vienna to spend a few days there with him but he wired he was leaving immediately and later wrote that he was disappointed and depressed by the sight of the postwar Vienna . . . *The Devil is a Woman* in the retrospective at Venice was the best film to be seen at the festival. Denise is well and happy and we both wonder when — if ever — you are coming here. Do so before we're put in bath chairs . . . You should have been in Venice. The festival films were mediocre but the weather was glorious and von Sternberg was a wonderful companion. We dined and shopped and drank a marvelous new beverage called the 'Bellini' (peach juice, orange, and champagne) . . . He talked of a story he had optioned and wants to film — I guess he's the greatest of the directors still with us."

From George Pratt of the George Eastman House in Rochester in reply to my inquiry about Louis Siegel, composer of the score for *Lot in Sodom,* one of the most remarkable music scores for a film ever written: "He died, apparently of cancer, in 1955. He was born in Rochester and when 11 was taken to Belgium where he studied under the violin virtuoso, Ovide Musin. At 16 he graduated with honors from the Royal Conservatory at Liege. He was a close associate later, in Vienna, of Leopold Godowsky . . . His obituary mentions only one composition, a short symphony (sic) called 'Nocturnal Rouge.' There is no word about his score for *Lot in Sodom.* In 1933 he was decorated by the government of Yugoslavia where he'd gone to conduct Bach, Beethoven and the violin concerto of the American composer, John Alden Carpenter. Hildegarde Watson (who played Lot's wife in the film) recalls listening to his rehearsals in Yugoslavia, which she was able to do as she was touring and singing in Europe at the time. 'He could play any instrument,' she told me on the phone yesterday. 'He was the finest violinist I ever heard, and his performance of the Bach Chaconne was unsurpassed.' In spite of the fact that he was a recluse, 'because he was almost pathologically shy,' 'Hildegarde said, 'He was a very, very great man.' Hildegarde recalled that he was a great friend also of Casals and at one time had gone to Spain and lived and worked with Casals, 'who was very fond of him.' Hildegarde said, 'Louis Siegel had the most marvelous musical mind I ever met.' She also recalled that the music for *Lot in Sodom* had so impressed someone in

Rome that he requested the score separately so that it could be performed there in concert."

And from Ben Abramson, the legendary Chicago bookseller: "Pale hands I loved beside the Shalimar . . . Where are they now?"

I'd taken my little daughter, Gretchen, to a press preview in New York of *Limelight*. The year was 1953 and she was ten years old. She met Chaplin after the screening and they had a pleasant interlude. The next day, Chaplin and his wife, Oona, left for Europe, and all that followed you know. Some 17 years later I wrote to him, offering to send him my first two books, on Sternberg and Lubitsch, thinking they might interest him. On April 13, 1970 he sent me the following letter from Vevey . . .

Dear Herman,

I think I can call you that for I have known you a long time, for you belong to the fraternity of the very rare ones — there's very few of us left!

Don't bother to send me copies of your books on Josef von Sternberg and The Lubitsch Touch, *because I have read them and enjoyed them both.*

Give my regards to your little girl who must be quite grown up by now. Tell her that I vividly remember that little girl on that mournful day of the press preview of Limelight.

If you ever come to this part of the world, you must call on us. We have a very comfortable house and a happy one and we should enjoy meeting you again.

Charles Chaplin

The following Associated Press dispatch from Copenhagen appeared shortly after the death of Chaplin:

CHAPLIN LEFT SCRIPT FOR
SATIRICAL FILM

COPENHAGEN—Charlie Chaplin left behind the script of a film satire containing so many detailed instructions that it is possible the movie still may be made, Danish poet-scientist Piet Hein said Sunday.

Hein was a close friend of Chaplin, who died Sunday in Switzerland at the age of 88. He would not disclose details of the script other than to say it is "a piece of powerful social satire, hitting out in a lot of directions."

Hein, 72, won Chaplin's friendship in the 1960s, after Hein had become internationally known for his epigrams, called "Grooks."

Hein said the film had reached the point of tentative casting and that Chaplin kept mentioning the film in letters.

In 1969, Hein nominated Chaplin for the Nobel Prize in literature, arguing that Chaplin was a great writer who used celluloid instead of paper.

Hein said of Chaplin, "What we see on his films is just an extension of Chaplin, the man, with all his human warmth and tolerance."

He said he probably could not put his feelings about the artist and friend better than he once did in a Grook dedicated to Chaplin:

> *The well you invite us to drink of.*
> *Is one that no drop may be bought of.*
> *You think of what all of us think of.*
> *But nobody else could have thought of.*

But even before Hein nominated Chaplin for the Nobel prize in literature, René Clair had done it — long before. Noting that Chaplin had written the scripts of every one of his films, shorts and features, Clair said that in their totality they made Chaplin a comic genius as a writer no less than Molière. And even before that, when the Tobis company, backers of René Clair's *A Nous la Liberté*, wanted to sue Chaplin for plagiarism for taking the conveyor belt sequence from it for his *Modern Times*, Clair refused to be a party to the suit saying he was not only flattered by it but that he owed everything he was as a film-maker to Chaplin. Tobis then dropped the suit and the Academie Française, of which Clair was a member, gained new luster by the incident.

. . .

Enshrined in my own cinema pantheon is a Mrs. Elizabeth Pavlukevich of an earlier day in San Francisco who was sentenced by a judge there (Justice Clayton Horn, s.v.p.) in the Municipal Court of that city, along with four other shoplifters, to see *The Ten Commandments* of DeMille and write an essay about the film, in penitence. Her four colleagues wrote glowing reports of the moral lesson they learned from it and were released forthwith. Not so Mrs. Pavlukevich. She took viewing the film as a punishment and wrote a review which so angered the judge that he slapped a $50.00 fine on her, saying, "You haven't shown any change of heart!" If only Mrs. Pavlukevich had not been such a good movie critic and Judge Horn had been a better movie critic, justice would have been better served.

MARLENE—A REMINISCENCE

". . . cet oiseau de haut vol, cette vamp des vamps . . ."

—JEAN COCTEAU

Do you know a book called *Die Frau nach der man sich sehnt?* (Published as *Three Loves* in English.)

It is a romantic novel by Max Brod, the Austrian-Jewish novelist and playwright, friend, literary executor and biographer of Kafka, and author of *Tycho Brahe's Way to God, The Redemption of Tycho Brahe, Reubeni, Prince of the Jews,* and a volume of poetry, *Neue Gedichte*. Spiritual probings into the genius of the Danish astronomer, Tycho Brahe, who paved the way for Kepler and other great astronomers and made their findings possible, philosophic works and poetical ones, all were at the root of what, by comparison, could be called even a trifling work, perhaps not much more than a *feuilleton*, the all but unknown *"romance sentimentale"* — *Die Frau nach der man sich sehnt* (The Woman for Whom One Yearns).

"Just a love story, then?" you will say. "So what?"

"Love may not be a very great thing," said Benhazigne, "but the rest, by comparison, is nothing at all."

"Alors!" you will insist. *"Na, und—?"*

Merely that this little love story of Brod was the source for the film by Kurt Bernhardt, made by Terra in Germany in 1928, that introduced to the world the very image of Marlene Dietrich that two years later was to stun that world in *Morocco* (not *The Blue Angel,* she was something else in that), but now become a vision, something seen as if by other than normal sight, a mental image, an imaginative contemplation . . . *fata morgana* . . .

Kurt Bernhardt? Who was Kurt Bernhardt? No one special, really, though he worked in Germany, France and Hollywood as film director. A list of the films he made would read like nothing at all — save for this one exception. Such odd things happen in that most bizarre of the arts — the films. E.A. Dupont was no great shakes as a director either, in Germany, England, or Hollywood — save for an absolutely stunning exception — *Variety*. Erle Kenton, a less than nothing Hollywood director of over a hundred films, once made a comedy, *Other*

Women's Husbands (1926), that could have been signed by Lubitsch. And so on. And Kurt Bernhardt made the film that introduced Dietrich to America under the title of *Three Loves* (which the English translation of the book was also called, when it was published here). All the other Dietrich films made in Germany before Sternberg discovered her for *The Blue Angel* were nothing at all. Whether Sternberg had ever seen the Brod-Bernhardt film is not clear. If he had, he must have seen nothing in it for him. The sluttish cabaret singer he was looking for was far removed from the image presented by the character, Stascha, in the Brod-Bernhardt film. That would come later, by which time he must certainly have forgotten (if he ever knew) the Brod-Bernhardt work. Besides which, Sternberg didn't need anyone else's vision of her to inspire him — he had his own, which he presented to the world in *Morocco* and which he sustained in five more films with her.

Opposite Dietrich played Kortner, the great Kortner, just as she was to have the great Jannings opposite her in *The Blue Angel*. The story of the Brod-Bernhardt film? Not much, as stories go, especially love stories. The Mayreder textile mills are bankrupt until the oldest son, Erwin, has a chance to marry the daughter of a rich banker which will save the Mayreder mills. By chance he sees Stascha and falls madly, hopelessly in love with her. She uses her chance meeting with Erwin to escape from Dr. Karkos, the man who is not only obsessed with her but, through circumstances, holds her in thrall. For a short while Erwin and Stascha find happiness together but only for a short while. Karkos finds them and takes Stascha away with him. She cannot follow. Let me end the story as the author, himself, puts it in a *précis:*

Erwin knows they've fled and when he learns this he looks for her everywhere, everywhere — wherever she could possible be. One day she meets him, by chance, on a street in Paris. They hardly know what to say. She invites him to her place, where she lives with Dr. Karkos. Karkos greets Erwin cooly, leaves Stascha alone with him, and goes into the next room.

No sooner are Stascha and Erwin alone then their words gush forth and rise so in their protestations to each other that the clamor brings Karkos running into their room. Stascha berates him for interfering, to which he replies grossly and shows Erwin the door, whereupon

Stascha throws herself on the door, barring Erwin's leaving, with her outstretched arms covering it.

"He's not going! I love him! Only him!"

As Erwin grabs Stascha to take her away with him, Karkos tries to prevent him and the two struggle, making such a din that the concierge soon arrives with a policeman.

Erwin is arested. In the detention house Erwin reads in a newspaper a few days later that Dr. Karkos has shot Stascha. The murderer is incarcerated in an insane asylum.

After Erwin's release, he would go every day to the house in which Stascha ended her life . . . to look at it.

The ex-officer and later textile tycoon Erwin Mayreder can today be seen, every day, by the Folies-Bergère, where he sells roasted chestnuts and watches bitterly the visitors to the Folies-Bergère. For they all seek happiness where it is not to be found, they all have not the slightest notion of that true happiness which is granted to be experienced just once. Happiness lies not in the erotic as offered by the revue in the Folies-Bergère, but in the boundless passion such as once burned in him for Stascha. That passion which knows no limits, which lifts one up to heaven and also flings one down to hell, that unconditional passion for which one dies, if necessary, which virtually asks for murder and death — so far has one been carried away by it — it is this passion, and this passion alone, which is the true happiness granted us.

Dietrich played Stascha, Kortner was Dr. Karkos and the young Swedish actor, Uno Henning (who had already appeared in Pabst's *Die Liebe der Jeanne Ney*) was Erwin Mayreder.

Now let us go back a while — to a real-life personage, one no less than Basil Zaharoff, the munitions billionaire, "Mystery Man of Europe," as he was known, riding the Orient Express one night when (and here let me quote how Harriet Van Horne described it in her review of E. H. Cookridge's book, "Orient Express"): "when a beautiful — and obviously distressed — Spanish bride came aboard. Her parents had just married her off to a deranged and depraved Bourbon prince, a cousin of King Alfonso. In the dead of night passengers heard a piercing scream. Into the passageway ran the ravaged bride, bruised and bleeding. Behind her glowered the prince (who was also a duke) brandishing a dagger. The bride burst into the first door opened to her — and it was Zaharoff's. 'Perhaps, Madame,' he said, 'I may have the honor to invite you to rest for a while . . .' That was the start of a love that lasted, without marriage, for 18 years. Duchess Maria, as she was known, bore Zaharoff three daughters. Together they travelled the Orient Express hundreds of times. Finally, when the Duchess was 55, the mad duke died in a Madrid asylum . . . The bride died, alas, 18 months later. Zaharoff rode the Orient Express one more time — in compartment 7, where he had sheltered the terrified girl in her torn peignoir. That night he asked to be wakened at 2:32 A.M., the precise moment she had fallen into his arms nearly 40 years before . . ."

In the book, Stascha runs away from the violent Dr. Karkos and meets Erwin in an elevator. (In the film they meet when he sees her on a train, with Karkos.) Erwin takes her from Karkos and for a brief while they again find happiness together but Karkos finds them, takes Stascha back and, not being able to win her back from Erwin, shoots her and ends his days in an insane asylum. Erwin is left alone, with only the memory of his great love — like Zaharoff. Did Brod pattern his novel after the romance of Zaharoff and Maria?

In the Fall of 1929, I received a letter from Dietrich. She had just completed *The Blue Angel* and was writing from Berlin-Wilmersdorf, where she lived.

"Dear Mr. Weinberg,

My friend, Mrs. Karman, has sent me notices which you were so kind in collecting and mailing to her . . ."

(These were the first reviews of a Dietrich film in America — reviews of *Three Loves*, the Brod-Bernhardt film — and they were already an augury of bright things to come.)

These are of great interest and value to me.

But I wish I could further impose on your kindness by asking you to please order for me the original newspapers in their entirety.

If I could get three of each newspaper, I would be very grateful to you.

I am enclosing name and date of the newspapers in hopes that this may help in getting the original papers.

Dear Mr. Weinberg

My friend Mrs. Kagman
has sent me notices which
~~you were so kind in~~ collecting
and mailing to her.
These are of great intrest
and value to me.
But I wish I could further
impose on your kindness by

This letter from Marlene Dietrich dates from 1930. It is a request for the New York reviews of her first starring film in the U.S. — *"Three Loves"*, a German silent film. She had just finished appearing in *"The Blue Angel"* and had signed with Paramount to come to Hollywood. I sent her the reviews, which were good, and met her at the boat (the S.S. Bremen) when she arrived. Her first film here was, of course, *"Morocco."* The rest is history.

asking you to please
order for me the original
newspapers in their entirety.

If I could get three of
each newspaper I would be
very gratefull to you.

I am inclosing name and
Date of the newspapers in
hopes that this may help
in getting the original papers

Again I say I am very thankfull
to you for kindness already extended
and hope you can help me now.

With my kindest regards
and hoping when I visit Amerika
I may thank you personaly

sincerely

Marlene Dietrich

Kaiserallee 54
Berlin Wilmersdorf

*Again I say I am very thankful to you for your kindness
already extended and hope you can help me now.*

*With my kindest regards and hoping when I visit
America I may thank you personally,*

> Sincerely,
> Marlene Dietrich

After I sent the newspapers, a large handsome portrait-study
of her by a Berlin photographer arrived, inscribed to me. (I have
never seen this picture published anywhere.) This was followed
by a *Blue Angel* postcard (like the one the students in the film
gloated over) saying when she would arrive in New York.

I met her at the North German Lloyd pier when she arrived
on the *Bremen* with several Paramount men in tow, on her way
to Hollywood to make her first American film with Sternberg.
She had given him a book to read on the voyage across, after
they'd completed *The Blue Angel*. The book was the novel
Amy Jolly (A Woman of Marrakech), by Benno Vigny, which
became the film, *Morocco*, a film as different from the novel as
The Blue Angel was different from Heinrich Mann's *Professor
Unrat*. After *Morocco* Garbo now had a rival.

Years later I met her (and Sternberg) again, at the Museum
of Modern Art in New York on the gala evening inaugurating a
retrospective of her seven Sternberg films. I recalled the inci-
dent of what the New York newspapers had said about her in
their reviews of the Brod-Bernhardt film. She smiled. "They
were right, weren't they?"

Then in 1968 I did a book about Sternberg, which was
almost as much about her, and this appeared in Paris via Edi-
tions Seghers in their Cinema d'Aujourd'hui Series. The fol-
lowing year an expanded English edition of this book appeared
in New York, via E.P. Dutton & Co. Sternberg had, in 1965,
already done his own book, *Fun in a Chinese Laundry* (The
Macmillan Co.). Again it was almost as much about her as
about himself. Some half dozen other books on her have since
appeared in England and America. "Everybody has had their
say," she said, not so long ago. "Now, I'm going to have *my*
say." And she is finally writing her own book about herself. It
will be a thing to read.*

---

*At this writing, Spring of 1979, word comes that G. Putnam & Sons, her
American publisher, rejected the book "for its lack of glamour," suggesting
she rewrite it or return the $200,000.00 advance they paid her. She returned
the advance, she wouldn't change a single word, the book appeared serially
in *Der Stern*, a Berlin magazine.

Marlene Dietrich and the author share a secret (1957) (Photo by Fred Stein) (Collection of the author)

To bring my reminiscence up to date, I had a telephone call from Maria Riva, her daughter. Was I still at the same address her mother in Paris had of me? Yes, I said. Augury of another letter from her? We had, in any case, after half a century, come full circle.

And finally, for the point he makes:

"Have you noticed there's an awful lot of rain in my pictures?" said William Wellman in one of his last interviews. "It's always raining in every one of my pictures. I don't know why — it just happens. When you see John Ford's pictures, they're all wind. He was wind-crazy and I was rain-crazy. It's an odd thing but I don't even remember putting it in. But I do love the rain. I love the rain especially if you're in love with someone. A rainy night in love is great."

Rain as a symbol of happiness on the screen ("Cinema is a marvelous weapon when it is handled by a free spirit," said Luis Buñuel. "Of all the means of expression, it is the one that is most like the human imagination . . . It's a curious thing that film can create such moments of compressed ritual — the raising of the everyday to the dramatic.") — at the beginning of *The Last Laugh* and at the end of Chaplin's *The Immigrant*, at the gathering of the jolly priests in Rossellini's *The Flowers of St. Francis* and the closing moment of Olmi's exquisite *I Fidanzati*, and even at the meeting of the lovers in my own little *Autumn Fire* that closes the film — but above all at the end of a non-film but what a book! — J.D. Salinger's *Catcher in the Rye* — as Holden Caulfield's little sister, Phoebe, in her blue coat, whirls merrily around on the carousel in the rain . . . blessed rain, bringer of life . . .

And what happened to the movies is the same thing that happened to our times. This, for instance, from the late James Thurber:

"Comedy didn't die, it just went crazy. It has identified itself with the very tensions and terror it once did so much to alleviate. We now have not only the comedy of menace, but also horror jokes, horror comics, and sick comedians."

And from George Cukor:

"I think this cult of ugliness, with everyone so unappetizing, is hideous. And to me, all this 'eroticism' is a bore, as though you were watching someone sitting on a toilet. There are other things. There's hope, disappointment.

Idyll in the rain (1974) (Photos by the author)

All the rest of the Western human scale has been neglected. We're human, after all. What *is* it to be human?"

And from Howard Hawks:

"You ask me why I don't make anymore films? I'll tell you why. Because American films now consist mostly of lousy, dirty, sick films — that's why."

And from Billy Wilder:

"The time for Lubitsch is past. It's a loss of something marvelous, the loss of a style I aspired to. The subtlest comedy you can get right now is *M*A*S*H*. They don't want to see a picture unless Peter Fonda is running over a dozen people or unless Clint Eastwood has got a machine gun that gets bigger all the time. It started out as a pistol and now it's a machine gun. Something which is warm and funny and gentle and urbane and civilized hasn't got a chance today. There is a lack of patience which is sweeping the nation — or the world, for that matter. Noël Coward would not succeed today. It's all tough guys. Today you have to have a dirty raincoat and be Columbo. They think it's very romantic . . .You are not going to buck audiences at two or three million a clip. What good is it being a composer of polkas if nobody dances the polka anymore?"

L'Envoi

"The only thing I can bring to this illogical, irresponsible and cruel universe is my love."

— Jean Renoir

"The boat of love has crashed on the rocks of everyday life."   — Mayakovsky's epitaph

And do you know who the last of the "People"is that I would like to offer in making my closing observation?

Toulouse-Lautrec — not the scandalous hero of fiction — but a man of dignity, generosity and wit. (He once said of Meissonier, the painter whom everyone else reviled for his fanatical "realism": "He worked very hard and anyone who works hard should be shown some respect.") "He had to wait nearly a month for his death," wrote Lautrec's biographer, Jean Bouet, "while the sun ripened the grapes on his estate and brought to a head the hatred of a world which could not forgive him for so lucidly describing its vanity and its putrefaction."

One lifetime isn't enough to encompass all that there's to be savored of it. One needs at least two — one to learn what it's all about — the other to benefit by it.

Just as I would have needed two volumes at least to tell all I wanted to tell, to describe many more observations made over half a century — a half a century is a long time. But no publisher is going to let you have two volumes unless you've got a Nobel Prize in literature under your belt. And unless you're an almost completely unknown writer from Peru, the Argentine or Tierra del Fuego, you haven't a chance, the way that's been going. The list of writers who never won a Nobel Prize in literature, from Tolstoi on, reads like a Roll of Honor, as witness: Chekhov, Ibsen, Hardy, Conrad, Mark Twain, Gorky, Sean O'Casey, Marcel Proust, Dreiser, Freud . . .

How, then, shall I close my book?

Since it appears in large measure to have been obsessed with women, let us quote Trimalchio (from *The Satyricon* of Petronius) who dictated his epitaph at one of his banquets:

"Here rests Pompeius Trimalchio. His beginning was small, but his end was great. Thirty million thalers he left behind, and he never listened to a philosopher."

Then, towards the end of the banquet he added, gallantly, "If women didn't exist, we'd consider all this —" and he swept his arm contemtuously to encompass the whole table on which glistened gold plates, goblets, tureens, a king's ransom in gold — "as so much dirt!" It is women who give value to life and who give things their value, according to what it means to them.

But that didn't keep him from saying, *sotto voce*, to Scintilla, "Did you know that Venus was cross-eyed?" There's a moral in that — think it over. But don't let it bother you.

I have come to the end of my book. If you have read "between the lines" (as we used to say), you will have noted that even better than my own distillations of what life has taught me is Blaise Pascal's axiom which has colored my life — the most beautiful to me of all axioms — "The heart has its reasons which reason does not know." And what this book is about more than anything else, is the pursuit of a hopeless quest: the quest for my youth. "Sometimes," commented Jean Cailleux, "for the lost innocence of childhood." (That's the wonderful thing about Salinger, of course. Brancusi, the great Rumanian sculptor, once said that when the soul of a child died within a man, the man became spiritually dead also). "One remains throughout life," continued Cailleux (in his essay, *L'Art du Dixhuitieme siècle*) "the man one was at the age of twenty . . ." (spiritually, of course, if not physically, alas) And yet we find Dean Swift saying, "No wise man ever wished to be younger." No?

Yet, as Keith says at the close of *South Wind*, "We are all at the mercy of youth."

But youth is not merciful, youth is pagan and paganism has nothing to do with mercy. Think back at your own youth — you wanted everything and with that "little bit o' luck" of which Doolittle sings in *My Fair Lady*, you got it or some of it — and that's what mattered.

The fact of it all is that youth must and will be served. What may it not accomplish? Like those characters in Chekhov would say, "Ah, youth!"

Little did they know what they were saying. Take the American college student of today. "Once upon a time Americans considered the college experience the best years of their lives," commented Harriet Van Horne in her review of *Campus Shock* by Lansing Lamont (Dutton, '79) in the New York Post of May 24 ('79). "Young people grew up in college. Their minds ripened, they fell in love, they laughed a lot. And they became Old Grads with misty eyes and swelling pride. But today! The college suicide rate has risen 250% in 25 years. The old campus green is now a small garrison state, spikey with security guards and alarm systems. Cheating is on the rise and civility in decline. Nervous breakdowns are taken for granted . . . a world of high tension, loose morals and fierce competition. He is, one gathers, awfully glad he's not young anymore . . ."

It is characteristic of the youth of today to be brutal lest it should be thought to be weak.

"One retains to the end of one's days the prejudices one formed in one's early years," Cailleux concludes. For better or for worse. He's right. After 50 years, I wouldn't change a single one of the prejudices I had at twenty. Life hasn't shown me a single reason to do so. Besides which, maybe I've talked too much . . .

Salinger was right. "Don't ever tell anybody anything," said Holden Caulfield in *Catcher in the Rye*, most exquisite of

The author, Etta and Gretchen

American books. "If you do, you start missing everybody."

And I do, I find I now miss many friends, some of whom I will never see again. I miss my first love, Erna, and my second, Etta — Gretchen's mother. Like Stascha, I had three loves — Erna, Etta and Gretchen — and I, too, have lost them all. Erna to another man, Etta to *"Hamavdil,"* the "Great Divider," and Gretchen who now has her companion.

Well, I haven't really lost Gretchen, only it's not like it was before. And just as I will remember to the end Holden Caulfield's little sister, Phoebe, in her blue coat going around and round on that carousel in Central Park, I will continue to think of those happiest days of my life when Etta, Gretchen and I lolled on the grass there, playing together. And each new day brings with it renewed hope that at night, in my dreams, there is the chance that we will be together again.

My book is all but done —
Remains?
The epilogue —
Very well, then, the epilogue.
Some news items among the many I kept throughout the
whole writing . . . item . . .

Welfare Mother Fined in $2.88 Theft

A Circuit Court judge in Danielson, Conn. has fined a
23-year-old welfare mother $10 for stealing $2.86 worth
of paper cups and plates for a birthday party for her
child. The woman, Maria Luberto of Plainfield, was
fined Monday by Judge Philip Dwyer after pleading guilty
to fourth degree larceny. The party supplies had been
taken from a Danielson shop on Aug. 19.

. . . item —

Paraplegic Mother Wins Custody of
Infant Girl

Philadelphia, Nov. 12 (UP) — A judge today awarded
Celestine Tate, a paraplegic, "full and free" custody of
her year-old baby and called Miss Tate "a symbol of hope
and inspiration of faith" to the handicapped.

"There are some people who say that if you will it, it will
be yours," Judge Edward Rosenberg of Family Court said
in issuing his decision. "And you have willed it."

The State Department of Public Welfare had charged last
spring that Miss Tate was incapable of taking care of her
daughter, Niya, who was then five months old. But to
prove her competence, Miss Tate undressed and dressed
the baby in court, using her lips and tongue.

Judge Rosenberg then affirmed her right to custody pend-
ing a reappearance in Family Court six months later for
re-evaluation.

"I have to commend you very much for your courage,
spirit and ingenuity," Judge Rosenberg said today. "You
have proven that physical endowments we have are only
part of the spectrum of resources that human beings
possess."

The alpha and omega of justice?

Of the human race.

And still about children . . .?

Always about children — that's how you tell about adults.

Like the two judges?

Like the two judges. I kept the clippings, along with many others which I have since discarded because they were too terrible. It's no use compounding the case one could build up against the human race. Were I to quote a score of items I had, not withholding the worst of them, I would not necessarily be making a stronger case so much as a more depressing one, and we have no need for that, even though I might have allayed them with occasional heartening items like the one about the paraplegic mother. But I kept the clippings up to the very last, thinking to use them, that they *must* be used — besides which it would have been no use to throw them away . . . I would still have remembered them. What has been seen cannot be unseen. Galileo says it in Brecht's play. You know, there was a little movie once, *The Mask of Dimitrios*, from an Ambler story, I think, with Peter Lorre and Sidney Greenstreet. I couldn't reconstruct the plot for you if my life depended on it but I never forgot the last line, spoken by Greenstreet, who's been shot and who staggers down a staircase holding on for dear life, as Lorre looks on appalled. Then he gasps out, as he reaches bottom, "You know what the trouble is? There's not enough kindness in the world." That's it — that's what it all resolves itself to. And I know that it's a pretty well-worn cliché to say but that's the way it is with old truths — they are called upon so often because they *are* true that they take on the patina of clichés. Very well. All truth is an edifice of clichés . . . and that's a cliché, too. Isn't it odd that so much of this book has been given over to diametrically opposed opposites, if you like, sex and children, though, of course, they are not so "opposite" except in the way they are used. We are skirting more clichés, aren't we? Sex and children. But the way they have been used makes a demarcation between them. Let me wind up our case by citing just two more — you see, I held out on two clippings, I couldn't throw them away somehow . . . and then we'll "call it a day" . . .

The following is from one of the papers that appeared during the New York newspaper strike (August 25, 1978 to be exact):

A mother's wish not to see her 8-day-old baby girl — and the letter of the law — were both observed yesterday when the infant was handed over to her thrilled adoptive parents at Booth Memorial Hospital in Flushing, Queens.

The mother, an attractive, unwed Manhattan secretary, agreed to give her child to a Nassau County policeman and his wife, some three months before the infant's birth, according to Eugene Hurley, attorney for the mother.

"She stipulated, however, that she didn't want to see the child. She was afraid she would be unable to give up her baby, after seeing her," Hurley said.

The Queens hospital, however, refused to release the baby unless the transfer was made to a child-adoption agency or the Bureau of Child Welfare, and was made in the presence of the natural mother, he added.

When the adoptive parents threatened to sue the hospital for custody, a special room with a ceiling-high partition was made available for the transfer.

The natural mother remained on one side of the partition, and didn't see the baby when she was brought into the room, Hurley said.

"The baby was asleep and there wasn't a sound," said Hurley. "I brought the child downstairs to the waiting couple. When I returned the mother asked me only one thing: 'What does the baby look like?'

"One thing I know is babies — I have six kids of my own. I told her that the baby is one of the prettiest I ever saw."

The mother, who was pleased with the arrangements, did not receive any money for handing over her baby, Hurley said. Neutral parties found the willing couple, who were unable to have their own child, the attorney said.

I cite this to show what a child means — it is all there, in that one item.

Well, not all. I'm writing this on the eve of Christmas and I have before me an illustrated news item showing excerpts from letters written by children to Santa Claus which the post office has gathered together in its central branch. Letters asking for gifts, for warm clothes, even asking "How is Mrs. Claus?" and reminding Santa to "fasten your safety belt" and promising to be good next year, etc. Readers may visit the post office, read the letters and take home as many as they wish to follow through. The post office received some 6000 this year. This is a more valid and meaningful figure than Xaviera's ridiculous 3500 sexual positions or the equally ridiculous 80,000 different Chinese dishes extant.

Withal, on the very next day appeared the following item in Earl Wilson's column in the N.Y. Post: "Regine's New Year's Eve price is a mere $350 a couple plus tips and taxes. That's for dinner and champagne for two . . . But Frank Valenza's elegant Palace Restaurant tops that: For a twelve course dinner with five wines, an 1880 cognac and cordials, only $600 a couple. But don't rush to make reservations. The Palace is sold out."

When one reads that at the gambling casinos in Atlantic City some $600,000 per night are wagered and lost by patrons each day and realizes that not a nickel of this ever goes to buy CARE packages for hungry children and adults around the world, what is one to think? Almost a third of the world's babies die before they reach the age of five, as reported by Arturo Tanco, president of the World Food Council. Did you know there are places in the world, (Asia, Africa, Latin America) where the infant mortality is so high, due to malnutrition, that mothers, realizing that their children won't live long, don't give them names when they are born? It's easier to bear the loss of a child when it dies, as it usually does, if it has no name, said CARE, describing such conditions it has met with and which it tries to alleviate. They beg for anything — $5.00 . . . $1.00 . . .

Charles Lamb, *On An Infant Dying As Soon As Born*, knew what it was, closing his bitter lines with:

> Mother's prattle, mother's kiss
> Baby fond, thou ne'er wilt miss:

Rites, which custom doth impose,
Silver bells, and baby clothes;
Coral redder than those lips
Which pale death did late eclipse;
Music framed for infants' glee,
Whistle never turned for thee'
Though thou wantst not, thou shalt have them,
Loving hearts were they which gave them.
Let not one be missing; nurse,
See them laid upon the hearse
Of infant slain by doom perverse.
Why should kings and nobles have
Pictured trophies to their grave,
And we, churls, to thee deny
Thy pretty toys with thee to lie —
A more harmless vanity?

From the New York Times, February 11, 1979: The Year of the Child

Suicides Among Young Persons
Said to Have Tripled in 20 Years

SAN DIEGO, Feb. 9 (UPI) — Suicides among teen-agers and young adults have tripled in the last 20 years, and children as young as 6 are now killing themselves, according to the director of a suicide prevention center.

"I think the major reason is the way our society has of alienating kids," Charlotte Ross, director of the San Mateo Suicide Prevention Center, said Wednesday.

Miss Ross, who was in San Diego for a conference on juvenile justice, said that the yearly suicide total for people between 15 and 24 years old was now almost 5,000. "We have validated attempts by kids as young as 6 or 7 years old," she said.

The reasons for suicide among young people are loss of a parent, a divorce, breaking up with a girlfriend or boyfriend and loss of self-esteem, health or faith, she said.

"So what at the end would our future historian make of it all?" concludes Christopher Booker in The New Statesman of Sept. 6, 1969:

"Perhaps he would not even be appalled at the hypocrisy of an age in which millions of magazines could be sold to supply the imagery for solitary vice, under the guise of

196

'art studies' or 'he-man' sexual liberation — a hypocrisy beside which anything in the Victorian age pales into complete insignificance. Perhaps he would in retrospect merely despair — at the thought that any collection of human beings could have so deluded themselves, led on by their gigantic illusion of sexual nirvana, while, beneath the dream, mounted ever higher the human wreckage of guilt, unwanted children, abandoned wives, abortions, and all the misery and despair of a galloping sexual instability.

"Perhaps he might conclude that the whole sex obsession had been notning more than a form of violent collective psychosis, which had come over a society trapped and made rootless by its increasingly technological environment, like rats in an electric maze. And he could, of course, be right."

A recent book, *Terroristic Shock:* An Exploration of Violence in the Seventies, by Michael Selzer, a former professor of political science and an authority on extremism, visits Studio 54 in New York, that "dancing, doping, fantasy market . . . Sartre's new hell . . . the ultimate ant-hill."

Like one of his constituents in the House of Lords said, summing up, following an address by Lord Rothschild on the perilous state of morality in a world all but torn apart by wars, famine and nuclear fission, its air and seas polluted — "Well, it's a reeling world, m'lords, and there's no finding true North anymore. But somewhere truth endures, blossoming out of the rocks. Look for it, it's always there — somewhere."

Not just somewhere — some*wheres* . . . many places; one has just to look for it . . . sometimes even in the smallest places, as in a letter I sent to Gretchen around this time . . .

Dear Gretchen,   6/25/79

The other night you said I was sentimental — I didn't deny it because I think it's a good quality. Just think how much better the world would be if *everyone* was sentimental . . .

If I'd said that one could become sentimental over anything — even an umbrella, say, or something like that, what would you have said? Smiled, thinking me soft in the head, perhaps? Well, here's one, in today's Times, Lost & Found Dept:

> LOST. Fri nite 6/22, Circle in the Square Theater, man's black umbrella, sentimental value. Reward. L. Schepp 757-8660

Isn't that sweet? If you were on trial, wouldn't you like to have someone like him for a judge, rather than someone who would think it perfectly silly to get sentimental over a lost umbrella?

Dad

* * *

It is good to see places where one has been happy in the past — to see them after many years and in different circumstances. The child is asleep in its rugs: that long, much-loved, much travelled coastline breasts its way up against the liner's deck until the town fans out — each minaret like the loved worn face of an earthly friend. I am looking, as if into a well, to recapture the faces of Hoyle, Gideon, Mills — and the dark vehement grace of E.

Ahead of us the night gathers, a different night, and Rhodes begins to fall into the unresponding sea from which only memory can rescue it. The clouds hang high over Anatolia. Other islands? Other futures?

Not, I think, after one has lived with the Marine Venus. The wound she gives one must carry to the world's end.

Lawrence Durrell: Reflections
on a Marine Venus (Penguin)

"Only artists are on the right track. It may be that they can give the world some beauty, even though to give it reason is impossible."

Georges Clemenceau

Copy of a Picasso print presented to sons of the Rosenbergs, by the artist.

Copy of a Picasso print presented to the sons of the Rosenbergs by the artist
. . . and inscribed by him, "To Michael and Bobby Rosenberg." (The
author's favorite of all Picasso's drawings)

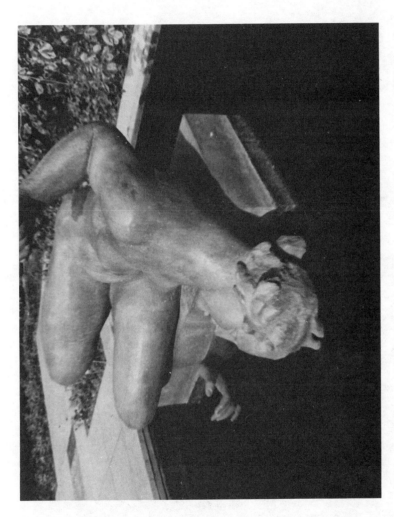

The River by Aristide Maillol (The author's favorite of all sculptures) (Museum of Modern Art — Photo by the author)

The author (1974) Copyright 1982 by Gretchen Berg

I'm done. I finished this in the winter of '79. Night is coming on and I'll go out now for a bit of fresh air after working on it indoors all day. As I put my notes away and dispose of others already used, one catches my eye. It is from Rilke, my old friend, Rilke, and it is so apt that I will close with it . . .

I call him my old friend because, though we never met, I've been reading him all my life and no friend of mine was ever closer to me than he was. His are the first words in a previous book of mine*, and now I call on him one more time, a last time, to provide me with all but the last words in this, my last book . . .

> Lord, it is time. The summer was
> too long.
> Lay now thy shadow over the
> sundials,
> and on the meadows let the winds
> blow strong.
> Bid the last fruit to ripen on the
> vine;
> allow them still two friendly
> southern days
> to bring them to perfection and
> to force
> the final sweetness in the heavy
> wine.
> Who has no house now will not
> build him one.
> Who is alone now will be long
> alone,
> will waken, read, and write long
> letters,
> and through the barren pathways
> up and down
> restlessly wander when dead leaves
> are blown.

But it's always been like that. More than a thousand years

**The Complete 'Wedding March'* (Little, Brown & Co., 1974).

ago, another poet, Chinese, Meng Hao-jan (689-740), des-
cribed it then —

> The trees are bare, the wild geese
>   have flown south,
> The north wind is cold upon the river . . .
> I see a lonely sail upon the horizon
>   and would like to follow it . . .
> I'm lost at the ford and wish to
>   ask the way,
> But there is only the vast expanse
>   of water
> And the night coming down . . .